A SLICE OF MAGIC

The Autobiography of Wyndham Beere, Co-founder of Abrakebabra Ltd

To Peter,

I hope you like my book a like minded platsman!

W

29/8/13

A Slice of Magic

The Autobiography of
Wyndham Beere, Co-founder of Abrakebabra Ltd

WYNDHAM BEERE

Contributing author
ROSALIND BEERE

BLACKHALL
PUBLISHING

This book was typeset by Ashfield Press for

BLACKHALL PUBLISHING
33 Carysfort Avenue
Blackrock
Co. Dublin
Ireland

e-mail: info@blackhallpublishing.com
www.blackhallpublishing.com

© Wyndham Beere, 2004

ISBN: 1 842180 85 1

A catalogue record for this book is available from the British Library.

Printed in Ireland by
ColourBooks Ltd

Contents

This book is dedicated to my mum and dad, Yolande and Stanley. My Mum gave me a sense of fair play and a love of people. My Dad, nicknamed "Bonnie", introduced me to the natural world all around us and to sport in all its forms. To both I am very grateful.

It is also dedicated to my mentor Augustus Kennedy Kisch, Managing Director of MEPC (Metropolitan Estate Property Corporation) Ireland, who taught me how to be a success in the property business, how to manage wealth and keep friends. I salute his memory.

Acknowledgements

MY DEEPEST THANKS to my daughter Rosalind, whose Masters thesis on franchising and academic case studies on Abrakebabra Ltd inspired me to write this book. Indeed Rosalind's work has laid the foundations upon which many chapters are based. I am immensely proud of my daughter, who so far has achieved a BA (Hons) at TCD and a MBS at UCD. Rosalind has recently begun her PhD in Business Franchising at Trinity College, Dublin.

A sincere thanks to all those who have helped, inspired and motivated me in my life. To my family, Shirley, David, Rosalind, Jeff and Gavin and to Shirley's family the Rosney's of Birr, Co. Offaly, a thank you for support in good times and in bad. To my brother Graeme, without whom *A Slice of Magic* would never have happened and his wife Margaret and family. A big thank you also to my brother Ian and his wife Joanne and family. Ian was a tower of strength to me at a difficult family time and for this I am forever grateful.

John Carthy of the Endorphin Release Clinic gave me back my health and I thank him and his staff for this gift. To Tony Keegan, who assisted me with the text, to Emma Dunne, who edited the manuscript, and to Justice Fergus M. Flood, retired, who contributed the Foreword, thank you. I am grateful to my solicitors David Doyle, who read the manuscript, and Cormac Gordon of Ivor Fitzpatrick and Mark Doyle of Actons, who have tried to keep me on the straight and narrow.

My friends Paul Kerr, Alan Sherwood, Des Kennedy, John Armstrong, Stuart Howart, Donal McCarthy, Niall O'Connor and their families have helped to keep my feet on the ground and I thank them.

Thanks also to the members and staff at Powerscourt Golf Club and the Stephen's Green Club; to Giorgio, Jeff and all the staff at the Unicorn Restaurant and the management and staff at Roly's Bistro and the Siam Restaurant at Monkstown. Thanks to the members of Dublin No. 1 Rotary Club and to the Committee and members of the Irish Orchid Society. A thank you to Pia Bang and family; John Mulcahy and Alan Bradley of Jones Lang LaSalle; Angel Brennan and Colm; John Brennan and family; Martin and Ann Whelan Devaux; Joe and Nell Beatty; Maurice Bryan of An Taisce; Dr Evelyn Moorkens; Clr Lettie McCarthy; EU Commissioner Charlie McCreevy and Noeleen; An Taoiseach

Bertie Ahern TD; Brian Cowan TD, Minister for Finance; Tom Parlon TD, Minister of State at the Department of Finance. To Arthur Godsil Headmaster and the staff at St Andrews College; the Headmaster and staff at The High School; and the Principal and Staff at the Sacred Heart School Mount Anville: thank you.

I am grateful also to Mark and Lynn Kennedy, Patricia O'Shaughnessy and the Doyle family, Ann Boylan and family, P.J. Gibbons (*Social and Personal* magazine), Dr Paul and Dr Sarah McAuley, Maeve Turner, Barry Sinclair (hypnotist), Denis O'Brien, Michael Harbourne, Sean and Ruth Lemass, James Roe of Roe Autocraft, Terry Mulally, Ambrose Glass, the staff and franchisees at Abrakebabra, our first franchisee Cheriff, Niall Fortune of Eddie Rockets, Nicky Toppin, Pat and Cathy Kenny, Gerry and Maura Ryan, George and Belinda Dyer, Caroline Barnardo of Barnardo Furriers, Allan Kilpatrick of Weirs, Audrey Taylor and Des Donovan, Derry and Mary O'Donovan, Dr Peter and Dr Aidan O'Boyle and families, Viv Gaine and Tom Williams, Jane Baker, Tom Day of Lisneys, Pat Gunne, Bill Cullen and Jackie Lavin, Padraig Hassett, Tony Leon, Paul Goode, Ethna and Michael Viney, Philip Chambers, Eileen and Tom Morrin, Nikki Carroll, Sean Gaffney, Berna Brennan, the staff and members of Birdwatch Ireland, Steve Wing in the Cape Clear Observatory, Pauline Bewick and family, Yona and Oliver Caffrey, Donie McDonald, Susan Sex, Debra Lambkin, Monica Carroll and family, Caroline Morahan (of *Off The Rails*), Conor and Liz Maguire, Simon at Hyperlink (who keeps my computer and me sane), the staff and management at Pronto Print, the Adult Art Class at Kilternan Community School and the Principal and staff at Our Lady of the Wayside School, Kilternan. Graeme and Wyn Beere, my relatives in New Zealand, who were a font of knowledge about my family history.

I thank also *Panorama* magazine; Larry O'Mahony and family; Dr Fiona Scanlon Moriarty, Eye Specialist; Donal McNally, Optica; Gabriel Dooley, Auctioneer; Colm Hayes; Noel Quinn; the staff and management of the Institute of Chartered Surveyors of Ireland; the Director, management and staff of the Botanical Gardens at Glasnevin; Management and staff of Powerscourt Garden Centre; Donal Pratt of Avoca Handweavers; An Garda Síochána, Stepaside; Des Kennedy, Stepaside PO; John Bowman, RTÉ; friends and colleagues in the Isle of Man; Gay Wright; staff at Access Travel; Doc and Monica Doherty; Jimmy Keating and family; Gerry and Patricia Kinsella; John Mulholland and family; Gerald and Clodagh Keane; Samantha Mumba; Ronan Keating; Maxi; Colm Meaney; Pierce Brosnan; Keith Duffy; David Went, Managing Director of Irish Life and Permanent; Noelle Campbell Sharpe; and lastly but by no means least Bishop Willie Walsh.

Many people have helped me over the years of my life and have contributed in different ways to the making of this book. I thank them now. If I have inadvertently omitted anyone they will know who they are and I thank them also.

Foreword

WYNDHAM BEERE, the author of this book, is a fellow member of the Stephen's Green Hibernian Club in Dublin. When he wrote to me and asked me to write a Foreword to his autobiography, *A Slice of Magic*, I readily agreed. On reflection, I wondered if I was competent to undertake this task. No one would ever classify me as a "literary bod".

Nonetheless, I set about the task and my first step was to read the text of *A Slice of Magic*. I found it a pleasant and interesting read although I have little knowledge of the commercial world.

At the outset of his autobiographical script the author has a chapter devoted to his surname and his family through the centuries. It is clearly a family with a remarkable record of being in the right place at the right time: for example, at the Battle of Hastings in 1066 it is recorded that Michael de Bure of Normandy was one of the knights that landed with William the Conqueror; later on they headed for Ireland with Strongbow and prospered thereafter.

The author gives an interesting account of the fortunes of his family in subsequent centuries including a distinct relationship with the clerical cloth and in succeeding years, adventures of generals and major soldiers in the British Army on foreign territory. His cousin, Thekla, was a distinguished member of the Irish Civil

Service under the Lemass Government. This is the background from which the author comes and his own success warrants that the Beere name is still to the forefront of all forms of activity.

The author was born in 1948 and he grew up in a banking environment, as his father worked in the Provincial Bank of Ireland. His secondary education was in St Andrews College and subsequently at The High School in Harcourt Street. At eighteen, he passed his Leaving Certificate. He decided that he would like to take a career in the world of business and obtained his first job in Ireland in Lisneys in Stephens Green as Leading Office Boy. In succeeding pages, Wyn sets out his career in the world of auctioneering, sometimes out on his own or sometimes as a member of the staff of one of the major auctioneers and estate agents. Whilst in Jones Lang Wootton he qualified as a Fellow of the Royal Institute of Chartered Surveyors.

In 1982 his brother Graeme and he inherited a fund from their deceased aunt and they decided to go into the fast-food business, having been fascinated for many years by the success of McDonald's in Grafton Street. His brother ran the first shop in Rathmines with the assistance of the author. In succeeding years the number of restaurants rapidly increased and each one was a success story, in particular one situated at O'Connell Bridge in Dublin. The name Abrakebabra became a household word in Dublin. This book is an interesting history of the progress of Abrakebabra as a fast-food empire. The name Abrakebabra in a striking green white and red logo flanked by two slightly tipsy palm trees ultimately encompassed 65 restaurants throughout the length and breadth of Ireland.

At the beginning their very success created its own problems, particularly with the increasing number of outlets, and it became more difficult to maintain tight financial control and quality management. At or about this time the author and his brother conceived the idea of operating by way of a franchise to an individual with a return to them and their company of 6 per cent of the earnings (net of VAT) of the individual outlet. This avoided the whole question of supervision and financial control of these varying outlets.

The essence of the franchise was that all outlets were built to a standard design, standard equipment ensuring a universally welcome and pleasant atmosphere with only one essential product, namely a kebab and soft drinks. The franchisee was obliged to purchase his supplies of lamb and all other products used in the restaurants from a nominated source, thereby controlling the standard. The author brought to this whole transaction and operation his experience in the commercial world of auctioneering and property management.

The concept of franchising was an immediate success and over a period of time made the author a very wealthy man. In recent times he has disposed of his interest in the franchising organisation for a very substantial sum. In the book the progress to that point of success is very openly and frankly detailed and is quite interesting to those concerned in commerce generally.

Having disposed of his interest, he is now undertaking the things that he likes to do including fishing, walking, generally relaxing, growing orchids and rearing butterflies.

A Slice of Magic is a pleasant and informative book that gives a very considerable insight into varying aspects of Dublin commercial life and into the problems involved in managing successful multiple outlets. I read it with interest and pleasure and I commend it to anyone who is interested in the world of commercial activity in Ireland.

THE HONOURABLE MR JUSTICE FERGUS M. FLOOD
Former Judge of the High Court.

Prologue

USPENDED UPSIDE-DOWN under a capsized canoe on the Monkey River in Belize, Central America, is, I am aware, an unusual way to begin a book ostensibly about kebabs and their impact on Irish late-night cuisine. But, I can assure you, when your head is three-foot below the water line, your booted foot is caught in the canoe and you are in crocodile-infested waters your life tends to pass through your mind rather rapidly. I had often heard that in near-death experiences, having run quickly through your life, you are inexorably drawn into a tunnel and propelled toward a blinding light. Well, the fact that I did not quite reach the tunnel was largely due to my prowess in swimming, particularly underwater. Over the years I had developed my lungs to a point where I could hold my breath for up to two minutes. But, notwithstanding this acquired talent, time was rapidly running out.

I kicked with my free foot again and again and at last made contact with the canoe. Using all my remaining strength I gave a final kick, freeing myself but severely damaging the tendons in my ankle. I surfaced. My companions and our precious cargo were safe and having righted the canoe we were able to continue to our destination without any further mishap.

When I returned home I thought long and hard about my life, my family and friends and what I had achieved. This book is the result of the labour of many, not least my daughter, Ros. My partner, Shirley, encouraged me to write the stories that she had personal experience of and others I had often told her. And my fellow Rotarian Tony Keegan assisted me with the text. I thank them all.

I will let my story tell itself, warts and all, because it is only in seeing all sides of a personality that you can understand the impulses that drive one forward, that give one the will to succeed. As far back as I can remember I have wanted to finish first, to triumph, even against the odds: finishing second was never an option that I readily embraced.

My life is not quite a rags-to-riches story, as the Beeres come from a comfortable background. It is, however, a tale of how hard work and ambition can overcome many obstacles; can cofound a chain of restaurants that at its peak had sixty-five restuarants, nearly double the number of McDonald's in Ireland; and can turn a £3,000 legacy into millions. It is a life that I have enjoyed and continue to enjoy, so sit back, take a deep breath and enjoy it with me.

The Beere name

THE BEERE NAME originated from the French "de la Bere" or "de Bure". Within a year of the Battle of Hastings (1066), which saw William of Normandy defeat the Saxon king Harold and conquer England, the foundation stone of an abbey to commemorate the great victory was laid. Dedicated to the Holy Trinity and in the care of the Benedictines, its high altar stood where Harold fell. The monks drew up a roll of the 375 commanders who had led the 5,000-strong force with Duke William on that great adventure. Michel de Bure from Normandy appears on the roll as one of the knights. This is the first reference to any member of my family in these islands.

The name crops up in Kent as Bere Forest at the time of the Magna Carta; in Hampshire where Henry III granted Peter de la Bere certain privileges in the New Forest; and in Somerset where William de la Bere was noted as a Knight of the Shire in 1300. To this day there is a town named Bere Regis in Dorset.

The Beeres, however, were a restless lot and, not content with helping William conquer England, some of them decided to follow Henry II to Ireland in 1169. As every schoolchild knows, Henry was keeping a close watch on Richard de Clare, Earl of

Pembroke (better known as Strongbow), who had been invited across by Diarmuid MacMorrough, King of Leinster, to help him settle a few old scores. Strongbow had been a little too successful and Henry did not want a rival kingdom next door.

The genealogist Sir Bernard Burke, who founded *Burke's Peerage and Gentry*, the bible of the nobility, assured my great-great-grandfather, the Reverend Gerald Beere MA TCD, that we were one of the oldest families in Ireland and, following the Norman invasion, had held extensive properties in Munster. One of the territories we acquired was a peninsula in West Cork/South Kerry that still bears our name: Beara.

It was at Dunboy Castle on the Beara peninsula, following the ill-fated Battle of Kinsale in 1601, that O'Sullivan Beare held out against the might of Lord Carew's army. Before the castle was taken he escaped and on 31 December 1602 he led about 1,000 of his followers on a 300-mile march, the like of which has not been seen in Ireland before or since. Harried and attacked by the English and some of the Irish, he led his men and women through the winter to the relative safety of Breffni O'Rourke's castle in Leitrim. Less than 100 people reached Leitrim; the rest perished on the way. Eventually O'Sullivan Beare and his faithful followers made their way to Spain, where he was rewarded with titles and land. The name still lingers, however, in Bere Island and Castletownbere.

After the revocation of the Edict of Nantes by Louis XIV in 1685, the religious tolerance that had been extended to French Protestants, known as Huguenots, by Henry IV in 1598 was revoked. They were allowed to leave France and many settled in Ireland, where they enriched the cultural and artistic life of the country. Among them were some Beeres, many of whom were goldsmiths; their marks are still preserved in the records. It is a matter of great regret to me that many of the family heirlooms that were in my keeping were eventually taken under unpleasant circumstances. But more of that anon.

In the eighteenth century the Beeres married into the powerful Butler family, headed by the Duke of Ormonde who claimed descent from Edward I. One of that Beere-Butler family was Colonel, later General, Sir Edward Butler. On 24 April 1794 he was one of six officers of the 13th Light Dragoons leading a reconnaissance force of 300 British and Austrian light cavalrymen, under the overall command of the Austrian General Peter Ott, when they ran into a strong force of French cavalry at Villers-en-Cauchies, near Cambrai.

Withdrawal was the most sensible option but they discovered that Austrian Emperor Francis I was nearby and any retreat would leave him in imminent danger of capture. At Ott's command Colonel Butler led his men in to attack the French, scattering them but then running into infantry, backed by cannon. Without stopping to think about their almost suicidal position against 12,000 men, Colonel Butler led his cavalry in, over-running the guns and breaking both the infantry and supporting French cavalry.

There followed a nine-mile pursuit that left some 1,200 Frenchmen killed, wounded or captured. There were only 66 casualties on the British side.

For his bravery and gallantry in saving the emperor from capture and leading his men to this stunning victory, Emperor Francis I invested him with the Gold Medal, Grand Cross and Chain of the Order of Maria Teresa and created him a baron of the Holy Roman Empire. Colonel Butler took part in many other engagements in the revolutionary wars against Napoleon and was afterwards made governor of the island of Mauritius.

My great-great-great-grandfather General Armstrong was not quite as fortunate as his near contemporary Colonel Edward

Butler. Having graduated from Trinity College Dublin (TCD), he joined the Duke of York's forces at Antwerp as a first lieutenant in December 1793. He was involved in a disastrous retreat during the winter of 1794–5 and embarked for home at Bremen. He took the surrender of French officers at Ballinamuck after their landing at Killala and the ensuing battle. He also helped put down the 1798 Rebellion. He did not become a full general until 1854, at the age of 92. I suppose perseverance pays.

Another Butler antecedent took his reputed royal lineage a little too seriously when he was high sheriff of Dublin. Apparently only royalty were permitted to drive a coach and eight horses through the streets. My ancestor took exception to this and decided that the way around it was to drive a coach drawn by seven horses and a bullock all the way from Tipperary right into Dublin Castle. No report on the reaction of the authorities survives but I like to think they approved of his ingenious scheme to get around the regulation. My own motto, "never take no for an answer", would certainly apply here.

The earliest reference to any Beeres in the Dublin directories is to Daniel Beere who was made a freeman of the Goldsmiths' Company in 1773, having served as an apprentice to his father. On 5 December 1776, at the age of nineteen, he was admitted as an attorney to the King's Inns in Dublin. He is listed in the Dublin directories from 1778 to 1830 and from 1779 was a "secondary" in the Lord Treasurer's Remembrancer's Office. He also had the title of Deputy Pursuivant of the Court of the Exchequer.

He married Margaret Butler of Ballyadams Castle, Tipperary, and in 1802 they moved into one of Dublin's finest houses: Mount Anville. Built on the slopes above Mount Merrion and affording magnificent views over Dublin and the bay, it is today an exclusive convent school for girls. In 1802 it stood in palatial splendour among extensive gardens and a deer-park that ran as far as the N11 and beyond Kilmacud. In later years Mount Anville became the residence of William Dargan the railway king, who built the first railway in Ireland – from Westland Row to Kingstown. The view from the tower was considered so good that in 1853 Queen Victoria visited the house to admire the vista and planted a "Regina" red oak tree that is still there. It is known as the Victory Tree, after her.

Unfortunately for Daniel the house was very expensive to maintain. The rent was £326.10.0 per annum and from 1820 onwards he tried to dispose of the house and to repay his brother-in-law, the aforementioned Colonel Edward Butler, for the latter's interest in the property. The house became a millstone around Daniel's neck and a source of friction between himself and Edward. Daniel even feared that he might be imprisoned for debt. Apparently his fears were well founded as, although he was in precarious health, he was obliged to flee the country and he died alone four months later, on 3 October 1831, at Havre de Gras in France, aged 74.

His son the Reverend Gerald Beere became a man of the cloth and married Mary Armstrong, the daughter of the afore-mentioned General Armstrong. Gerald was a graduate of TCD and rector of Kilbiny, County Westmeath, and Adare, County Limerick, and a prebendary of Limerick Cathedral. He had eight children and part of the family lore quoted above comes from a letter Gerald wrote from California House in Adare, County Limerick, to his daughter Margaret in California on the west coast of the USA in 1868. The letter was in reply to a request from her for information on her family.

One of Gerald's sons, Gerald Butler Beere, followed in the family tradition by joining the military. He became a captain in the 62nd Regiment, married a widow, Matilda Sophia Wright (*née* Brady) and immigrated to New Zealand on the *Helvellyn* in 1853. He was appointed captain of the 4th Waikato Militia, found work as an engineer and built Berefort, from which the district of Beerescourt took its name.

Another son of Gerald's, Alexander Beere, married Alice Maunsell, a cousin of the Wyndham Quinns, earls of Dunraven. My somewhat unusual Christian name originates from this. Alexander's brother Holroyd was a school friend of the third earl and when he decided to follow his brother to New Zealand the earl and countess provided character references, which are still in the possession of the family. We also have a *Book of Common Prayer* presented to Holroyd by his Sunday school teacher, the Countess of Dunraven.

New Zealand was not a random choice for the Beeres: their uncle on their mother's side, Robert Maunsell, had gone there in 1835 as a missionary. He became a noted Maori scholar and a contemporary rated him as the best there had ever been. He spent many years translating the Bible from Hebrew and Greek into the Maori language and was awarded an honorary doctorate by TCD in recognition of his work in this field.

Robert and his wife Susan established schools to educate the Maoris and set up a mission at Waikato Heads. He helped to collect signatures for the Treaty of Waitangi in 1840. The treaty was the founding document of New Zealand and set out the rights and responsibilities of the newly arrived immigrants from Europe and the indigenous Maori people. Over 500 chiefs and representatives of the colonists signed the treaty. Robert Maunsell conducted the first church service in the new town of Auckland in 1841 and became archbishop of that city in 1869.

Back in Ireland yet another son of the prolific Reverend Gerald Beere, Nenon, married a Miss Thomasina Brady, the daughter of another reverend gentleman, Thomas Brady. Nenon, who acquired his rather unusual name from the Armstrong side of the family, was a member of the Royal Engineers and was my great-grandfather. And so, after a long journey of military expeditions and missionary endeavour, we have finally reached the twentieth century.

I like to think that courage and perseverance, whether on the battlefield or in spreading the faith, are a hallmark of our family. Nowadays such qualities are more rare than they used to be. But they can certainly be useful when it comes to business.

CHAPTER 2

Beeres and Nelsons

I SUPPOSE THE KINDEST thing you could say about my grandfather the Reverend Hugh Clement Beere MA TCD is that when it came to his family, his church and life generally he took matters seriously. Hugh Clement, the son of Nenon and Thomasina Beere (née Brady) was born on 16 May 1876. He was fifth of six children, four boys and two girls. Hugh Clement was educated at Rathmines School and obtained an MA from the Divinity School in TCD. He was ordained into the Church of Ireland in 1899 and served as curate in Clara and as rector of Laracor from 1903 to 1933 and as rector of Kilmessan and Galtrim, County Meath, from 1933 to his retirement in 1942.

My grandfather married Eileen Stanley in September 1903 and they had four children: my father, Hugh Stanley, Eileen Marjorie, Nenon John and Florence Thomasina, whom I knew as Auntie Florence. The tradition of naming the eldest son Hugh continued down to my generation: I was named Hugh Wyndham and my eldest son is Hugh David.

The church into which Hugh Clement had been ordained had been disestablished some 30 years previously, with all that entailed. It had been removed from its *de jure* position as the dominant force in Irish life and its government had accepted that the Church of Ireland would play second fiddle from then on to their Roman Catholic brethren. Nonetheless, it was still very powerful and what it lacked in numbers, compared to Irish Roman Catholics, it more than made up for in wealth. The tithes and all they represented might have gone but the Church of Ireland congregations contained most of the landed gentry and leading merchants and industrialists in the country.

There had been a tradition that Beeres would serve the faith and the Reverend Hugh Clement's father and two of his brothers were clergymen, not to mention the cousins who had carried the Protestant religion to the Antipodes. To put the best gloss on it, the certainty Hugh Clement Beere lost when the Church of Ireland ceased to be the state church was replaced with a conviction that his children, at least, would follow the true path.

He had high standards and, unfortunately for us, my father did not measure up to his father's ideals at all times. In fact, if truth were told, my father, Hugh Stanley, was rather the antithesis of his father, in that he took a more relaxed view of things and was not at all attracted to the life of a reverend.

My grandmother Eileen Stanley had taught in St Andrews College before she married and was a quiet and kindly lady – in contrast to her husband, who definitely knew how the world around him should be run. When I knew her she had Parkinson's disease and she and her husband were living near us in Booterstown.

Hugh Clement and his wife were well-respected members of the community in Laracor, Kilmessan and Galtrim and I remember him driving an open-topped Riley, being very well turned out and giving me a Christmas present of a wooden crane. I probably caught some of my love for classic cars from him. One of the great interests of his life was butterflies and he introduced my father to the pleasures of being a lepidopterist. My dad in turn brought me into the countryside when I was a child and explained to me the differences between butterflies and moths and how to identify the species. This love of butterflies has remained with me all my life and, while I have mixed feelings about my grandfather with regard to many things, I do thank him for being instrumental in opening part of the natural world to me.

My grandfather's brother the Reverend Francis Beere married and was rector of Kells, County Meath. His daughter Thekla is probably one of the best known of our family in the last century. My father always said she was the brains of the family.

Thekla June Beere was educated at Alexandra College, Dublin, and at TCD, where she took a moderatorship in Legal and Political Science and an LL.B. In later years she was a governor of Alexandra College. Thekla won a Rockefeller scholarship and travelled extensively in the US. She entered the civil service in the statistics branch and transferred to the Department of Industry and Commerce in 1939, where she became assistant secretary in 1953. She was an acknowledged expert on shipping, transport and labour matters.

During the Second World War Thekla worked closely with her minister, Seán Lemass, to solve the supply problems of wheat and turf. After the war she represented Ireland at many major international conferences. In 1959 she was appointed secretary of the newly created Department of Transport and Power under the late Erskine Childers, afterwards president of Ireland. She was the first woman in the history of the state to hold such a post. In 1960 Dublin University conferred an honorary degree of Doctor of Laws upon her.

She retired as secretary of the Department of Transport and Power in 1967 and three years later was appointed to chair the newly established Council for the Status of Women. As a tribute in 1984, the then Minister for Women's Affairs, Ms Nuala

Fennell T.D., presented Dr Beere with a leather-bound copy of the first epoch-making report of the commission.

Thekla, like my father, was a great walker and I owe my love of nature in part to her. In 1931 she was one of the founders of An Óige, the Irish youth hostel organisation, and I was delighted to be asked to say a few words at the unveiling of a plaque in her honour at the new International Youth Hostel in Glendalough in 1999.

Thekla never married. She used to say that she couldn't afford to. What she meant was that, as women had to retire from the public service and all jobs in the private sector on marriage, she would stand to lose a lot of money given her grade.

She was always interested in the arts and was a great friend of the artist Cecil King. She had many of his paintings in her Stillorgan home and seeing them in a domestic setting, rather than on gallery walls, certainly whetted my appetite for some original paintings of my own. Unfortunately she never left any to me: they all went to her sister June, who lived in England and was chronically ill. I was, however, always invited to her cocktail parties where government ministers, high civil servants and people from the business community rubbed shoulders with people from the artistic and outdoors world. At that time I was property manager with MEPC, who owned Stillorgan Shopping Centre. Invariably she would complain about shoppers throwing rubbish into her garden. It did no good to assure her that my duty was to ensure that the tenants kept to the obligations of their leases: I had no responsibility for garbage. When Thekla died we lost a woman who made a truly unique contribution to Irish life.

My mother's father, Donald Nelson, was completely different from my other grandfather, the Reverend Hugh Clement.

Donald had been in the Scottish Fusiliers during the First World War and was quite happy to show a little boy the shrapnel still imbedded in his calf. He also confirmed for me that true Scottish men do not wear anything under their kilt. We have a wonderful photograph of him in his full regalia, topped off by a busby-type hat and plume. My grandmother was an Englishwoman and they had a large family. Donald worked for Burtons, the well-known tailors, and around 1920 he was sent to manage their Jersey branch. While he was there my mother, Yolande Victoria Odette, was born and two years later Donald was transferred to Dublin to open Burtons' new shop on the corner of South Great George's Street and Dame Street. Donald and his wife liked Dublin and they rented a house in Sutton, on the north coast of the county. He stayed on there after he took early retirement from Burtons.

He then turned his hand to hiring out limousines and had a fleet of cars, including Rolls Royces, that he provided for weddings, funerals and special events such as the Horse Show and the races. More evidence, if need be, of fancy cars in my genes.

He was doing quite well for himself in this business when the Second World War intervened. Because of petrol rationing he was unable to run his cars any more. Everything had to be sold at a loss, including the Rolls.

By this time, Donald and his wife and family had moved to Clifden, a lovely Regency house on Leinster Road West, near Kenilworth Park in the south suburbs of Dublin. I remember a very impressive flight of granite steps up to the hall door and a huge back garden. Donald was not a man to give up easily. He converted a shed in his back garden and, with the help of his wife and sons, started an upholstery business, specialising in supplying licensed premises. I can recall, on a visit there, seeing my grandmother wipe the varnish stains off her hands before she greeted me. The business has continued into the present generation as Nelson and Son and, in addition to upholstery, they now supply fitted furniture. It is now run by Donald's son Bobby and his family.

It was quite common in the 1940s for people to rent houses rather than purchase them outright. Donald Nelson was no exception to this practice and the annual rent on Clifden was very small. Another son, Teddy, bought his parents' family home from the landlord and soon after they had to find a new abode. The same son repeated the manoeuvre with premises that his brother had in Rathmines, to which the upholstery business had been transferred. Again they had to move on. I came across this cousin some years later in Australia and was sad to see that he had not put his money to good use.

As I was growing up I saw a lot of the Nelsons and always found them to be open hearted and welcoming. They were not at all like my other grandfather, who was somewhat of a throwback to Victorian times. Christmas Day was always spent at the Nelsons, with a wonderful spread of food and great fun. They were a big family and certainly knew how to enjoy themselves. My father, on the other hand, never looked forward to these Christmas forays. I supposed the Nelsons teased him a bit and he was not the centre of attention – the position that he usually occupied at home.

"There were far too many of them," my father told me. "I couldn't take them all on."

CHAPTER 3

Bonnie and Yolande

HUGH STANLEY BEERE was born on 21 September 1905 and spent his early years in the rectory at Laracor, County Meath. He loved the open air and took full advantage of the countryside around him from an early age. Sport came naturally to him; he was fast, had a good eye and was good looking. He attended the local parish school until he was old enough to be sent to St Andrews College, at that time on St Stephen's Green in the centre of Dublin and where Dr Imrie from Scotland was headmaster. My father was not a boarder, however, and stayed with his grandmother Stanley on Anglesea Road in Ballsbridge. Initially he travelled by tram from Donnybrook and when he was old enough he cycled the two miles each day into school. From an early age, due to his striking fair hair, he was known as "Bonnie" and the names Hugh Stanley appear only in formal documents. Although he tried to study as hard as he could, it was evident from an early age that his heart was not really in it. His great love was sport and at that he excelled.

These were turbulent times for Ireland and during the Easter holidays when he was ten the 1916 Rebellion was fought across the green from St Andrews in the College of Surgeons. Troubles such as these and the ensuing War of Independence passed Bonnie by and he progressed to be a college champion at swimming, tennis, cricket, boxing and athletics. He was also adept at riding with the local hunt, shooting and water polo. However he excelled at rugby.

St Andrews, founded in 1894, had won the Senior Schools Rugby Cup twice, in 1906 and 1911, but in 1921 they were pitted against cup-specialists Blackrock College in the final and were given little chance of winning. Blackrock were so confident of success that they had booked two tram cars to take them on their anticipated triumphant return journey from Lansdowne Road. Bonnie Beere was in his fifth year at the college and was picked at centre for the final XV. Whatever about Blackrock, few outside St Andrews gave them any chance of defeating their mighty opponents. As the game progressed Blackrock took the anticipated control but they could not cross the Andrews line. In the second half Andrews scored two tries to clinch the game and Bonnie Beere gave the final pass that resulted in the winning try. The excitement can only be imagined but the Blackrock trams went home quietly and the Andrews boys, who had made no provision for victory, had to hire a number of taxis to take them back in triumph to St Stephen's Green.

My father received a year's free schooling for his part in that epic win and in the following year he was a member of the Senior Schools Rugby Cup team that completed a double by defeating Blackrock again in the final. In the second final Bonnie was again in the thick of the action and, once more playing in the centre, gave the penultimate pass to the winger Dunbar who went over for the winning try. Bonnie was a hero. There are not many colleges that, even to this day, can boast of such a double. The St Andrews line-up in 1921 had a cosmopolitan look to it: Imrie from Scotland, son of the headmaster, was at full back and one of the forwards and Henderson, who was over six foot, was from the US.

With three others from the winning St Andrews side, Bonnie

was chosen to play at centre for the Irish schools team that defeated the English schoolboys 12-0 at Lansdowne Road in 1922 and Dad went over for a try.

Following in his father's footsteps, Bonnie went up to Trinity in the autumn of 1923 and set about securing his moderatorship. He wanted to be a teacher and saw that as a splendid way to continue to indulge his passion for sport and the outdoor life in general. There were a lot of distractions at Trinity, however, particularly for a good-looking young man who excelled at whatever sport he turned his hand to. He had to knuckle down to his studies, his father informed him, or his support would be withdrawn. Unfortunately for my dad he did not knuckle down quickly enough and the Reverend Hugh Clement decided that my dad's younger brother, Nenon, was a better bet in the academic stakes. In those times a son could do nothing to reverse such a decision. College life was expensive and it would not have been viable for my dad to support himself through four years without his father's stipend. Fathers made decisions and, according to the culture of the time, sons acquiesced.

The bank was deemed suitable and a position was found for my father in the Provincial Bank's head office in College Street. The old banking hall is now a feature of the five-star Westin Hotel. Bank clerks, at that time, were held in high esteem and if you had any liking at all for the work involved you could have a nice life indeed. The bank would readily pay for your membership to rugby and golf clubs and there was a good social life. Whether because he was forced into it against his will or he just did not like the work, Bonnie hated the bank. His demeanour was not improved when, as was the custom, he was transferred from Dublin to a country branch. He had joined Wanderers after leaving college and felt the best way to impress the Irish selectors was by playing under their noses in Lansdowne Road. In Adare, where he had been sent, there was no one to impress. Notwithstanding this perceived handicap, he did manage to be capped for Leinster and for Munster after he transferred to Garryowen. He did the usual round of country branches and always said that the bank had conspired against him getting an Irish cap at senior level.

After a number of years he returned to the bank in Dublin and took digs out in Sutton. Many young men, in particular, not having the self-catering skills that their more adept sisters had had instilled into them, needed a home from home when they had to leave their parents' nest due to work commitments. Digs provided such an environment. Depending on your luck, they provided such home comforts as a bed, an evening meal and breakfast; you could get your clothes washed, dried and ironed; and you could have somewhere to sit in the evening. You paid for this, of course, and it provided a nice income for many families and pocket money for others. In my father's case there was an added benefit: his socks were darned for him too. Although he was quite delighted with this arrangement, he could not make out who was doing the darning and didn't want to ask, lest it cease. From his point of view, all his time out of the accursed bank should be taken up with either watching or participating in sport of some kind and darning socks was not really on his agenda. Nonetheless he was curious and returning early one evening in 1940 he was just in time to see the young lady of the house placing the neatly darned socks on his bed.

It was love at first sight for my dad, who obviously knew a good woman when he saw her, and the feeling was returned by Yolande Victoria Odette Nelson, the daughter of the house, who became Mrs Hugh Stanley Beere the following year. There was a considerable age difference between them, my dad being thirty seven and my mum seventeen when they were married in September 1942. She had just left Alexandra College and there was also the rather inconvenient fact that my dad had been engaged five times before he proposed to Yolande. Making doubly sure, he confessed to her that he was also "a bit of a playboy", which I think may have been a slight understatement. It did not faze my mum, however, and their marriage of 29 years was a very happy one.

By 1941 the Second World War had been going strong for two years and in Ireland the Emergency was in full swing. Everything was in short supply and to have a permanent job in the bank must have been a tremendous asset. Not according to my father, however, who loathed every minute of it. The newly-wed couple set up home in rented unfurnished accommodation on the top floor of 8 Belmont Villas, off Belmont Avenue in the south Dublin suburb of Donnybrook. Number 8 was very conveniently situated for my dad, overlooking, as it did, Mary's Tennis Club, also known as Percy's. His home was a short stroll from the Andrews swimming-pool at Montrose and another short walk from Lansdowne Road. He was in his element.

As I have already mentioned, my mother was born in Jersey, in a farmhouse in the Valle des Vaux ("Valley of the Cows"). When I decided to write this book I went back there and was struck by how peaceful a place it is. The whole valley is alive with wild flowers and daffodils and there are orchids along the river that runs through it. There was just one farmhouse nestling in the valley and it looked to me a beautiful place to be born. She was just two when her family came to Ireland and she underwent all her education here. My mother, Yolande, was considered a great beauty as a young girl and that beauty lasted well into her middle age. Bonnie and Yolande made a really striking couple.

As I read back through this chapter, I cannot help but notice that it is practically all about my dad, Bonnie. But that is a reflection of how our family was. My father was a larger-than-life character and even now I can still recall the advice he gave me.

"Nobody remembers those who finish second," he would say. He would pause and then add, "Don't be that person, Wyn. Always come first."

I have done my best to live up to his motto over the years. While I was not able to emulate his feats on the rugby field, due to a catalogue of injuries, I did manage to excel at many other sports.

In the relationship between my mother and father, she was the rock on whom you could always depend and he was the soaring eagle who would bring back news of great deeds from far-flung corners of the sporting world. She was always there to talk to, a shoulder to cry on, and she was the one with the easy jokes to make life more bearable. She always understood and was a bulwark against life's troubles.

In many ways it was an extraordinary relationship, with such a difference in age and personality, but it worked. My mother and father needed each other and they complemented each other in the best possible way.

When I was in secondary school, I remember my father bringing me across the road from the St Andrews playing fields at Montrose, where RTÉ is now. We went into a large house and he introduced me to a beautiful woman. We had a cup of tea and they chatted for a while. After we left he told me, sadly, that he was once engaged to the lady we had just met. He went on to say that, unfortunately, they had to break their engagement when it was discovered that she could not have children. From the way he spoke I felt that there was still a spark between them after all the years. It made me feel a bit uneasy at the time but I now understand that love can endure, even through the most painful circumstances.

CHAPTER 4

Early years

I WAS BORN on 6 April 1948 and baptised as Hugh Donald Wyndham in St Mary's Church, Donnybrook. Dr David Solomons was our family GP but my dad's pal Karl Mullen, the hero of that year's Irish Triple Crown victory, delivered me. Coincidentally Karl Mullen's grandson Cian O'Connor, who won a gold medal for Ireland at the 2004 Athens Olympics, attended the same school, Kilternan National, that my own son Gavin attends. Although I am the eldest in the family I was not the first-born: a brother named Graeme had preceded me but died soon after birth from a brain haemorrhage. My parents used the same name for my youngest brother, who was born ten years after my own birth. The first Graeme's death coloured my family's attitude to me as a young child: they were very protective and anxious that I should remain well and healthy. I am glad to say that all through my life I have enjoyed excellent health apart from some self-inflicted injuries, largely due to sporting and other outdoor activities.

From my earliest years the only incident of note was when my mother, having brought me to nearby Herbert Park in my pram, nodded off in the summer sunshine. The pram rolled down a slope and I was deposited in the ornamental pond among the ducks and swans. Luckily enough a passing park keeper saw my plight and rescued me from drowning. This was my introduction to nature and, although I cannot say that I have a clear, if any, recollection of the event, it had a beneficial effect. I say this because one of my earliest memories is of being placed face down by my dad on a pouffe in our living-room. In front of me on the floor was an illustrated book of swimming instructions and I was expected to execute the strokes under his supervision. I do not know if this was a reaction to the Herbert Park incident but he was a good teacher and not long after I had learned how to walk I was a proficient swimmer.

Although when it came to anything sporting my father was the lead figure, as a young boy I naturally spent most time with my mum. When I was two, a little brother, Ian, arrived and I had at last an on-the-spot playmate with whom I could have adventures.

School reared its ugly head when I was only five and I was not too interested. My mother, however, had other ideas and I was dragged, screaming and kicking, down Morehampton Road to Park House School on the corner of Herbert Park. It is now an An Óige youth hostel but at that time it was a leading girls' school that took in boys up to first class. P.J. Southgate, headmaster of St Andrews, whom I was to meet again soon enough, lived at the end of Belmont Avenue and was often on hand to assist my mother in conveying me to my new school.

Park House was a lovely school and although I was reluctant to go I have only happy memories of the establishment. Miss Catt, who was in charge of the junior babies (I'm sure there is a more politically correct name now), sized me up pretty quickly and gave me a patch of the school garden in which I could grow flowers. I still remember the thrill I felt when, having planted and watered them, I saw the seeds germinating and turning into lovely colourful flowers. I had seen my mum and dad doing something similar in our garden at home but to be able to actually do it myself, when I was so little, was a revelation and in its way a life-changing event. I had also often accompanied my father to his plot where the Riverview Sports Club is now in Clonskeagh. Being a rector's son he quite naturally grew his own vegetables and our family were always self-sufficient in that regard. But now I was growing flowers myself and that was different.

After a couple of years I was on the move again – this time to St Andrews College, which had moved from St Stephen's Green to Clyde Road in Ballsbridge. By now it was a family tradition to go there and it was certainly the nearest Protestant school. Due to his advancing years, the headmaster, P.J. Southgate, was beginning to lose control of the school. At the time, however, I was glad to be in the company of lads of my own age and particularly enjoyed the sporting aspect of the school curriculum.

Muckross Park, an exclusive school for Catholic girls, was quite near our house. Extensive parklands with mature trees that provided a great environment for birds' nests surrounded it. My father told me that, as birds couldn't count, if I found two eggs in a nest it was perfectly all right to take one for my growing collection. I suspect that he was not entirely accurate and that, being very keen sighted, birds are likely to know how many eggs there are in their nests. Having said that, one must also consider that the cuckoo gets away with planting her eggs in other birds' nests, often disguising them by changing the colour of the shell. In any event, I collected birds' eggs, which is now illegal, and perhaps my love of nature and my desire to protect it is a guilty reaction to my youthful indiscretions. I am not alone in this as a good friend of mine, Maurice Bryan, chairman of the Irish Wildbird Conservancy, afterwards Bird Watch Ireland, confided to me that he had a similar hobby when a young boy.

Our next-door neighbour in Belmont Villas was a Mr Farren from Switzerland. He taught me to play chess and had a stunningly beautiful daughter, Ray Ray, who, although only two years older than I was, put my religious convictions to the test. Ray Ray, Jim Kent, Keith Richardson and I were playing some action-packed game in our garden when Ray Ray decided to re-enact the rather fiery end of Joan of Arc. Being only eight, I was not quite *au fait* with the details of that French saint's life and death but agreed to participate because I really fancied Ray Ray and, if truth be told, was a little in awe of her. But she wasn't always as good as she looked. As the game progressed it became evident that one's religion was to play an important part in it. Ray Ray demanded to know what religion I was.

"Protestant," I replied proudly. No doubt the Reverend Hugh Clement would have approved.

"Right," Ray Ray replied, "you are for the stake."

She proceeded to tie me to the nearest tree. When she asked my fellow St Andrews schoolmate, Keith Richardson, what religion he was, he immediately replied that as he went to Gonzaga he must be Catholic. My cries alerted my mother to my plight and she came and released me from the impending torment. I don't know where Ray Ray intended to obtain the matches from but she could be such a bold girl that I do not doubt she would have followed through on her plan.

When I was seven I was given a present of a new bike for my birthday. It was a two-wheel model with stabilisers and now I was able to whizz up and down our little road and even explore around the corner. I was beginning to spread my wings. Unfortunately an older boy took severe exception to my new-found mobility and determined to do something to curtail it. He took my brand-new bike and proceeded to dismantle it, nut by nut and bolt by bolt, until it lay in ruins on the pavement. In retrospect it was some achievement and he must have had a lot of time on his hands and a few spanners. At the time, however, I was distraught and ran crying to my mother, who uttered the fateful words, "Wait until your dad gets home."

At about 5.30 p.m. Dad arrived home from the bank and was not at all happy when he was confronted with a mass of metal, mudguards, bolts and handlebars. He went in search of the culprit and managed to track him down. In the forthright fashion that he was well known for, he explained the position carefully to the young miscreant and set out the options facing him. Later that evening a shamefaced lad was sitting on the pavement outside our home, surrounded by bike parts. By 9 p.m. he had managed to reassemble the vehicle. Not only had I my bike back but also, funnily enough, I never had any trouble from that quarter again.

By now it was 1956 and our time in Donnybrook was coming to an end. My dad was quite happy to continue to rent 8 Belmont Villas because of its proximity to the sporting venues that he frequented. But the landlord wanted us out because, as the first floor where we lived was unfurnished, our rent was controlled and, with the passing years and the impact of inflation, in real terms it had become very low. To persuade us to move he installed African tenants in the ground floor of number 8 but the result was not quite what he had hoped. We got on very well with the medical students and one of them used to baby-sit us.

My mother, however, wanted a house of our own. Many of her friends were purchasing semi-detached houses in the newly built suburbs and she could not see why someone like her husband, with a good job in the bank, could not afford something similar. But Bonnie was not interested in approaching the bank for a loan at the preferential rate for employees. He wanted as little as possible to do with the place and lived for the day when he would be shut of it altogether. Yolande was not a woman to be thwarted in her ambition so she set about finding a suitable house and obtained a loan from the County Council to purchase it. Confronted with the inevitable, Bonnie agreed to the purchase and we moved out to what at the time was nearly the country, to 8 Glenomena Park behind P.V. Doyle's Montrose Hotel on the Stillorgan Road. You will have noticed that the number eight occurs in both addresses and that I was eight when we moved. I have always considered eight to be my lucky number and it has recurred many times in my life.

Glenomena Park was completely different to Belmont Villas in that fields surrounded it and we had a whole house to ourselves. As the house was only two years old there were many young families on the road and lots of lads to make friends with. The as-yet-undeveloped UCD campus at Belfield was on our doorstep and Sandymount Strand was just down the road. The house was built by Waites and sold on to us by the Besslers, who had brought the huge cranes into Dublin port. Being an engineer, Derek Bessler had installed many features into number 8 that we benefited from. These included hidden lighting under the banisters, a kitchen window unique to our house, a vine in a green house, a trapdoor under the fire grate that caught the hot ashes and a clothesline on a pulley that you could operate from just outside the back door. The Besslers had built a split-level bungalow in Dalkey with a stunning view of Dublin Bay. We became firm friends and often visited them there.

Although it had been my mother's idea to move out to Glenomena Park, my dad was very happy there. The 46A bus brought him into town and he could walk to the St Andrews pool and the beach. When we were there only two years my brother Graeme was born and our family was complete.

I made many friends among the young lads on the road, including Alan Sherwood. Alan and his brother Derek were living across the road from us when his mother became very ill and had to go into hospital for a year. My mother took the two brothers to live with us and we became like siblings, doing everything together. I met Alan again in Old Conna Golf Club and we remain very good friends. My mother was a very kind-hearted woman and was always on the look out for any people that she could help.

Around this time my dad was involved in foiling an armed robbery at the bank. He was in the Capel Street branch one day when an armed robber came in and demanded cash. Having filled his sack, the robber then proceeded to make his getaway. He reckoned, however, without Bonnie, who vaulted the counter, sprinted up the street after him, took him down in a rugby tackle and retrieved the stolen cash. The guards arrived soon after and the robber was handed over. If Bonnie was expecting praise and perhaps a little reward from the manager of the branch he was sorely disappointed. The manager called him into his office and admonished him for putting his life at risk in the service of his employers. The clincher was: "You are not insured, you know, Bonnie. If you had got yourself killed there would be no compensation."

A sobering thought, but one that had not occurred to my impetuous dad.

After my grandfather retired as rector of Kilmessan and Galtrim he lived for a while in Meath and then bought a house on Trimleston Road, which was within walking distance of our home and between the sea and us. His wife Eileen, my grandmother, had died in 1955. Relations with Bonnie had remained the same, although my dad often helped his father by chopping wood for him. But he also used the same axe to provide wood for our family. I am sure other factors were involved but the axe was the straw that broke the camel's back, so to speak.

On Christmas Day 1956 my grandfather appeared at our home demanding to know where his axe was and why his son had not returned it to him as he was meant to. Words ensued from both sides — I suppose it was the inevitable result of years of frustration on both of their parts — and my grandfather stormed off with his axe. After that there was a definite coolness between them that had not been resolved by the time of the Reverend Hugh Clement's death on 9 January 1958.

As the eldest son, my father was entitled to expect that his father would have provided something for him in his will. Unfortunately this was not the case and, apart from a few sticks of furniture, the estate was divided between his three siblings. It fell to my grandfather's executor, Thekla Beere, to impart the bad news to my dad. While he never held it against her, he was very angry at this unexpected turn of events and I remember him tearing up the small cheque he received from her when the furniture was sold. He was standing in the hallway of our home when he shredded it and I can still see the small pieces of paper fluttering to the floor. So many unspoken dreams were destroyed at that time and it was many years later before some effort was made to heal the breach caused by my grandfather's will.

CHAPTER 5

Growing up

B Y THIS TIME I had moved with my school pals into the secondary part of St Andrews College. I was very happy there and particularly liked the sporting aspect of the school curriculum. I became school champion at swimming and sprinting and was also on the rugby team. Notwithstanding my best efforts, however, I did not excel at rugby to the same extent as my dad. I tried hard but constant injuries tended to inhibit my progress, although I was always on the first XV for my age.

The college was not prospering and its headmaster, P.J. Southgate, appeared to be part of the cause. Many felt he should have retired years before. He had taken to falling down the stairs in the morning and a number of reported incidents led one to believe that he was not quite the man he had been.

One of these involved a young salesman for Hodges Figgis who had made an appointment, one morning, to introduce the headmaster to the most-up-to-date schoolbooks on the market. The headmaster was busy when he arrived and he had to take his place in a queue. The young man was pleased to note that each interview did not take very long and soon he was in the headmaster's office. Imagine his surprise when he was grabbed by the collar, placed face down over a desk and the cane applied to his posterior by the headmaster, who had been administering punishments that morning. Onlookers attest that, when the individual concerned had extricated himself from his predicament, he ran down Clyde Road and never again tried to interest the school in the latest editions. Nowadays, such an incident would bring a suit for damages and a resultant scandal, but things were different then.

There were good teachers at St Andrews and I was lucky to have one of them for mathematics and geography. Jimmy "The Bull" Duke made the most difficult problems appear simple. With maths, in particular, he showed us how to approach problems and to cut away all the peripheral details and get to the nub. Thanks to him I have always been very good at these subjects and this facility was a great help when it came to my career as a chartered surveyor. Jimmy Duke was from Canada; his stepson Arthur was in my class and we became firm friends. When Jimmy Duke took over as headmaster the standards in St Andrews improved and it became once again one of the leading colleges in Dublin.

By this time my dad, Bonnie, had acquired a second-hand Model Y Ford. This was especially useful for summer holidays and I remember many happy weeks in my mother's family's caravan, parked in the corner of a field behind the sand dunes at Donabate. Wildlife abounded all around us and a corncrake nested in the field beside us. Each day I watched the bird go to its nest, concealed among the stalks of corn. Unfortunately I was there for the harvest as well and witnessed the destruction of the nest and its contents. This memory stayed with me and I am glad to say that I have been able to play a part in changing the habits of farmers at harvesting time. They now begin their work from the centre of the field outwards, allowing the birds and their young to have an escape route.

When we were in Donabate Dad often brought Ian and I for walks through the fields, introducing us to nature in all its variety. One day the three of us were walking through a field of cows when it transpired that not all the cattle were female: one – and a big one at that – was male. The bull charged us and Dad shouted to us to run to the right while he attracted the attention of the beast by waving his arms. When he was certain that it was going for him, he ran as fast as twenty Park Drive a day would allow him and barely managed to scale the gate before the animal hit it. We had scrambled to safety by this time and were observing the unfolding drama with fear and trepidation. It was a close-run thing and scaling the gate nearly killed Bonnie, never mind the bull.

There were only two years between Ian and me and inevitably there was competition. Being the sort of person I am, not to mention the fact that I was older, I nearly always won. In collecting butterflies, for instance, I was the tops. I still have my *Observer Book of Butterflies* from 1955 that details our captures and there in black and white is "Wyn 6–Ian 2". The fact that I was seven and he was five and that I could therefore run faster to catch them did not enter into the equation. I was better and that was it.

There was an occasion, however, when our struggles for supremacy nearly ended in tragedy. We were motoring along in the Model Y Ford with Dad at the wheel and Mum in the back. Inexplicably Ian and I were sharing the front passenger seat. I use the word "sharing" in its widest sense because neither of us wanted the other to sit comfortably on the seat. Both of us wanted it for ourselves. The car was speeding along, probably at about 30 m.p.h., when suddenly our manoeuvring resulted in the passenger door swinging open and Ian sailing out, clinging to it for dear life. My dad stopped as quickly as he could but Ian was very shaken and so was I. Car doors in those days were hinged to the column between the front and back of the vehicle and Ian could easily have been killed by our antics. Words were said, we quietened down and the Sunday trip to the seaside was completed without any further mishap. There were no seat belts in those days and children were allowed to occupy the front passenger seat without hindrance.

Swimming took up most of the days at Donabate but come the evening the local shop was turned into a disco and all the young people in the vicinity descended on it. Elvis was all the rage and I thought I looked really cool in my tight jeans, slicked-down hair and sideburns. At least Valerie Foster agreed with my notion of my appearance because one night she kissed me, thus opening up a whole new area of endeavour that had to take its place among my other activities, such as swimming, running, rugby, butterflies and other outdoor pursuits. She also taught me how to inhale a cigarette, which resulted in my collapsing. Valerie's interest in me didn't last too long but, having tasted the previously forbidden fruit of her lovely lips, like all hot-blooded young males I wanted more of it: how to get it was the perennial problem.

While I pondered this dilemma I was also in the local scout troop, the 25th Mount Merrion on Fosters Avenue. Dad had been scoutmaster of the Donnybrook troop and we hiked the length and breadth of the Wicklow hills together. Dad knew every inch of Wicklow and had been leading hikes there since the 1920s. Many of our hikes began from the old scout hut in the Powerscourt demesne near Enniskerry. From there we would tramp on, often over-nighting in the folds of the hills. Around the campfire I learned to play a few chords on the Spanish guitar from Ian McQuillan and as my teenage years advanced I graduated to an electric Fender guitar. I have many happy memories of the fun-filled days and nights with our troop. I am reminded of my youthful adventures nearly every week because the old scout campsite can be clearly seen from the eighth tee of the new eighteen holes at the West Course at Powerscourt Golf Club, of which I am a member.

Back in 8 Glenomena Park there was a problem. Our breadman was not too well and, as my mother had discovered, he lived on his own and was finding life difficult. Yolande suggested that he move in with us as a paying guest and she would nurse him back to health. He did and some months later he was back on the road in his little electric van, gliding around the estates dropping in loaves, batch pans and turnovers. He liked the set-up in 8 Glenomena Park so much that he stayed with us and, like so many other people, became a part of our extended family. In the meantime he had inherited money and, as he had no immediate use for it, he offered £1,000 of it to Bonnie as a long-term loan. Whereas my dad would never think of approaching the bank for a loan, he had no difficulty accepting it from our newfound friend the breadman. In fact Bonnie, his bank training coming to the fore, insisted on writing out an IOU for £1,000 and handing it over. It was not required but Bonnie felt better when he had done it.

John Greene, the breadman, was integrated into our family to such an extent that he began to accompany us to the Nelsons for family events, including the Christmas celebrations. One day in general conversation he asked Bonnie to repay the loan. Yes, it had been long term, with no specific repayment date, but things had changed and he wanted it back now. On further investigation Bonnie discovered that John wanted to loan the money to one of Yolande's family, the Nelsons. Not expecting to have to repay the money that quickly, Bonnie refused, quoting the long-term nature of the transaction. John was having none of this, however. A court case ensued, the IOU was produced and the judge had no option but to direct Bonnie to repay the money immediately. I think that he had to go to the dreaded bank but the loan was paid back, our breadman moved out and the Nelson's got a new paying guest. Relations were strained between the two families for a while but with the passing of time matters returned to normal. My father told me never to put anything in writing unless the other party insists, and then only having shown it to a solicitor. This was good advice from the school of life's experiences.

At this time, every available minute was spent outdoors. I had been observing the fishermen on Sandymount Strand and had noticed how they laid out their hooks and lines at low tide and then went back at the next low tide to harvest their catch. It seemed to be a great way of catching fish so I got my dad to obtain some twine from the bank that they used for tying up bundles of notes and, having cadged some hooks from a couple of the older men, I laid out my lines. I dug up the lugworms myself and walked out as far as I could follow the retreating ride. Twelve hours later I was back again, running across the wet sand, and I was surprised and delighted to discover that I, or rather my lines, had caught four sea bass. The next day it was the same story and soon I was feeding the road from my endeavours on Sandymount Strand. My dad said that anyone who married Wyn would never go hungry and, as events have turned out, he was right.

When I was not catching fish I was snaring rabbits in Belfield and bringing them home for the pot. One day I went to where I had set my snare and was dismayed to discover that the rabbit had not been strangled by the wire and was only half caught. The disturbing part of the event was that I interrupted a fox that was feasting on the rabbit's foot. After this I discontinued my rabbit-snaring activities and confined my foraging to fish and hunting with my pellet gun.

One day in Dornden Park, at the back of the Tara Towers Hotel, as I was aiming my pellet gun at a wood pigeon, a fox trotted by my feet, quite unconcerned, no doubt on his regular patrol. I was so taken aback that I didn't react quickly enough and so lost another trophy.

Another big excitement on Glenamena was Mr Who, who came to live on the corner. To us he was an exotic character and, as we didn't know his name, we christened him Mr Who because it seemed, somehow, to be appropriate. Lovely young ladies would lounge in deck chairs in his front garden and, better still, they would give us sweets and money to go away. The excitement reached a crescendo when the Gardaí raided the house and took all its occupants off in the Black Maria. It turned out that Mr Who was on the run from the English police, who wanted to interview him in connection with a bank robbery in London. We really missed the money, sweets and girls – not necessarily in that order.

At St Andrews I had won the Hazlett Cup for the 200-yard sprint and I was school champion for the high jump and the long jump. I also excelled at swimming and became Leinster champion for the crawl, butterfly and breaststroke. I had joined Pembroke Swimming Club and was on their water-polo team with John Mulvey of Mulveys Hardware store in Ranelagh who has remained a good friend. Swimming and running took up a great deal of my time and swimming, in particular, has remained a pastime all my life. Hardly a day goes by that I do not swim half a dozen lengths of the pool in front of my home, most of it under water.

Often, after school, I would walk down to College Street and help my dad count the cash before coming home with him. The queues at his counter were always a bit longer than the others. He had a friendly word for everyone he dealt with and although he never liked the bank he certainly enjoyed meeting and chatting with its customers. I usually received a florin for my assistance with the cash and I put it with the rest of my savings because I really wanted to get a motorbike as soon as I turned sixteen and was eligible for a licence.

All through my years growing up I attended rugby matches with my dad in Lansdowne Road and Bective's ground in Donnybrook. The remarkable thing about our attendance was that, no matter what match was being played, he never paid to gain admittance. The procedure was identical each time. We would approach the ground along with the rest of the supporters and when they headed for the stiles we would veer slightly to the right or left, depending on the topography, and Bonnie would discreetly knock on a door. The door would open slightly, visual recognition would be established and the steward would utter the usual words: "Ah, sure it's Bonnie. Come on in and is that the young fella? Isn't he the spit of you?"

Sometimes there would be two of us, as Ian would be brought along also. It did not seem to matter. Bonnie knew everybody even remotely connected to the sporting life of Dublin and everybody knew and liked him. We watched club matches, inter-provincials and even internationals without paying a penny. You would never get away with this now. Or would you? I like to think there are still Bonnies out there who can knock on little doors and have them opened quietly. I hope there are.

CHAPTER 6

Later on

B Y NOW I was sixteen and, through delivering newspapers on my bicycle, had built up sufficient capital to acquire a Puch 50 cc moped. This was a great little conveyance with a two-stroke engine and you could pedal it as well. It got me through the paper round a lot quicker and now that I was mobile I could explore further the places that my dad had brought us on weekend trips. It was a bit slow going up hills but once it got to the top it whizzed along. The feeling of freedom that having your own motorised transport gives you is wonderful. Pillion passengers were a bit of a difficulty because it didn't have the power to really carry two at any reasonable speed and pedalling was hard work. So, as soon as I could, I invested in a Honda 50 that, although it had the same engine size, packed more punch.

At St Andrews my attitude to learning was that it rather interfered with my sporting and social life and was something to be endured. I did not find the curriculum difficult but found my other activities more interesting.

Alexandra College was the equivalent girls' school to ours and a lot of the lads in St Andrews had sisters and cousins there. Not having a sister myself and our school being boys only, at the time, I was reliant on the other lads for introductions. Chemistry was one subject that never really caught my attention and

Wednesday afternoons, when it was scheduled, were really boring. There was also the added factor that the Alexandra girls had a half-day on Wednesdays and could be found having coffee in various emporia on Grafton Street. The lure was too great for a few of us young bucks and most Wednesdays we would throw our bags over the back wall of St Andrews into the lane behind and follow them ourselves. There was no check in the afternoon on attendance and we got away with this for months.

With my dad's assistance I had graduated to a Moto Guzzi 110 cc bike, which was really powerful and could go up hills without any bother, even with a well-built girl on the pillion. One Wednesday afternoon two mates and myself bunked over the wall as usual and headed for Grafton Street for our routine assignation with the Alex girls in Switzers' coffee dock, where Brown Thomas is now.

As we walked along St Stephen's Green I saw the most beautiful sight: a brand new Moto Guzzi with a 150 cc engine lying casually against a lamppost opposite the top of Kildare Street. It looked so inviting that the temptation to try it out became too much for me and I felt compelled to take it for a short spin. This was a seriously bad idea and I would not recommend anyone to follow my example. Anyhow, off I sped. The exhilaration of having such power under me was too much and I did not return the bike as quickly as I had intended. When I eventually left it back, an hour or so later, its loss had been reported by its owner who worked just across the road. Inquiries led directly to me and my father and mother were asked to attend at St Andrews College forthwith.

Quite naturally, the college authorities took a rather dim view of my activities and after some discussion my parents were asked to find another school for me. This was a major disgrace for my dad, as he loved St Andrews and was dismayed that his eldest son would bring such opprobrium on our family. My younger brother Ian was two years behind me and still remembers the shock he experienced at being told that I had to leave. Jimmy Dukes, who had been my maths and geography teacher, was upset at the turn of events and did everything possible to smooth my passage to a new school. I was in fifth year at the time and was due to sit the Leaving Certificate the following year. There could not be a worse time in which to change schools.

Calls were made and letters written and eventually it transpired that The High School in Harcourt Street was prepared to take me, so in September 1965 I was entrusted into the care of Dr Reynolds, its headmaster. Although I knew no one in my new school, a few factors worked in my favour and helped to ease my passage into that very different environment. One of these was rugby: I was a very fast winger and was immediately snapped up for the first XV. Another was that I was put sitting beside John Armstrong. John was, and is, a great guy and he looked after me and introduced me to the other lads: in no time at all I was part of the group. I have always been grateful to John for his care of me at this personally vulnerable time and we remain good friends to this day. John qualified as a chartered accountant and is now managing director of Taylor Signs. We meet most weeks and chat about life's good times and bad and I know that in John I have a true friend whose advice I have always found to be very sound.

Another plus for me was that The High School was a much better school academically, at this time, than St Andrews and there was peer pressure to study and do well in the coming exams. My sporting and other extra-curricular activities took a back seat and over the next nine months I applied myself to doing well in the Leaving Certificate. My efforts paid off and when the results came out the following year I not only passed but also obtained honours in maths, English and art. I would never have achieved such marks had I remained in Andrews. It is strange how events can have an effect on your life. I have learned over the years that it is not the events themselves that can assist or damage you: it is how you deal with them. In this case what seemed an absolute disaster had turned into, not quite a triumph, but certainly a success. All my life I have tried to see how I can turn a setback into something positive and to try to not repeat the same mistake.

With studies completed and the whole summer ahead of me before the results of the Leaving Certificate would come out, I did what many a young man before me had done: I headed for London. I was eighteen, tall and strong and I wanted to earn a few bob to set myself up for the year ahead. Like all mums, my mother was worried about my moral and physical welfare in such a cosmopolitan environment and arranged that I should stay with her sister Joyce. My worries were of quite a different kind: I wondered what the girls over there were like and how you would go about meeting them. I need not have worried because in the meantime I had perfected my guitar playing and had discovered to my great delight that women were particularly attracted to a chap who could strum a few chords and carry a song. My dad had encouraged me to persevere with the guitar, as you could carry it anywhere, unlike a piano. As usual, he was right.

Auntie Joyce took some getting used to. Although she was married and had two children of her own, she did not always appreciate the social necessities that went with being eighteen and in London during the swinging sixties. My sojourn there was short enough but unlike many others I do remember actually being there, though some memories are a little blurred.

I obtained employment in a builders' providers in Hemel

Hempstead. The job entailed ensuring that the various building sites had sufficient blocks, bricks, planks, mortar, nails, plaster and whatever else they required. In the evenings, instead of practising my guitar, I spent my time picking splinters out of my hands and trying to wash the concrete dust off. On the building sites I came across a wide variety of people, from Irish navvies straight off the boat to old hands who had come over after the Second World War and were struggling to keep up with their younger compatriots. There were also a number of ex-convicts, festooned with tattoos of every kind imaginable. It was a great finishing school and an introduction to the real world for which I am very grateful.

I was earning about £20 a week, which was a fortune in those days, and although Auntie Joyce had to be given a few pounds for my lodging and another few pounds to send to my mum I still had more than enough for myself. At the weekend, pubs, dances and parties beckoned and the rumour about the guitar attracting females proved to be pretty accurate. The previous year a few friends and myself had formed a band that we called The Young Shadows, after the somewhat older quartet that originally backed Cliff Richard. We had got a couple of gigs in Marian College in Sandymount and other such venues so I was well used to performing in public

My friend Jimmy Dunne had also come over to England and was working in Walton on Thames. One weekend I decided to spread my wings and head for Walton. I slept on the floor in Jimmy's room and we had a great time. The social life in Walton was nearly better than in Hemel Hempstead and I enjoyed Jimmy's company so much that I invited him back to stay with me the following weekend. On the Friday morning I mentioned to Auntie Joyce that my friend Jimmy would be coming to stay for the weekend and I was dismayed when she adamantly refused to allow him to cross her threshold. This was an immense shock to me because I had grown up in a house where friends and soon-to-be friends were always welcome to come and stay. My mother was the most hospitable of women and I could not believe that her sister was so different. Jimmy was on his way so I could not put him off, even if I wanted to – which I didn't. We ended up sleeping on the floor in a girlfriend's flat and, while it was a very enjoyable weekend, I was terribly embarrassed that I was not allowed to return the hospitality that I had been shown.

Given the attitude of my aunt to my friends, I felt I really could not stay any longer in London. So after eight enjoyable weeks, I returned to Dublin in time to receive my good Leaving results and to see what fate had in store for me in the employment and romantic world.

CHAPTER 7

On the rebound

BACK HOME another aunt, Eileen, arranged an interview for me with Lisney, the leading firm of auctioneers and estate agents, with offices on St Stephen's Green. I was somewhat taken aback to discover that the starting salary was a mere £3 a week, which, compared to what I had been earning in London, was a bit of a come down. It also transpired that although I had got the job I couldn't start for another six months, when the position of leading office boy would become available. I had been attracted to the estate-agent business because I perceived that one could be out and about a good deal and would not be confined to a desk. I had already taken a position with General Accident, which had its offices just around the corner on Dawson Street. If I had needed any confirmation that life tied to a desk was not for me I certainly got it there. Row after row of desks stretched out behind the public counter, with clerks beavering away at mountains of paperwork. I spent as much time as possible in the filing room and got to know a lot of the smokers, such as Ronnie Coates and Aubrey Shaw, quite well. I also got to know Gordon Cadle, on of the insurance inspectors.

After six months I started as leading office boy, in charge of photocopying, in Lisney. I was not long there when I discovered the existence of expenses. This is a word beloved of employees and not highly regarded by senior management. In my case, being tied to the photocopying machine, I couldn't generate any expenses but after a while I worked out a way around this difficulty. Some months after I started a new young lad came along and took over my onerous duties. I rapidly let it be known that I was willing to show any property in Dublin north or south at very little notice. Not surprisingly my offer was taken up by many of the sales staff and I found myself whizzing around on my Moto Guzzi, clocking up the miles. It was a bad week when my expenses did not exceed my wages by a substantial amount.

I liked the estate agent's work and after about a year I left Lisney and went to work for Paddy MacKeogh in Andrew Street. Paddy had a more selective method of attracting clients. Each day he would look through the death notices. When he came across a death on what he termed a good road he would note this information in his diary. A "good road" would be one in Foxrock, Dalkey, Rathgar, Donnybrook, Ballsbridge, Clontarf, Howth or Sutton: the kind of place where prices would be good and commissions high. After a respectable amount of time had passed, one of his lieutenants would be dispatched to interview the surviving spouse or executor with a view to discovering if a sale was contemplated. In many cases no sales were in the offing but in a good number of instances there were and Paddy snapped them up. It was an unusual way of doing business but it certainly worked.

By this time I had met my first real girlfriend, Jean Bibby. We had met at the St Andrews Marquee Dance beside the school swimming-pool and immediately there was a spark between us. With my Moto Guzzi I was able to go anywhere I wanted and most weekends we headed off to Brittas Bay with sleeping-bags. Another favourite haunt of ours was the disused Harcourt Street railway, which is now used by the Luas. The good times continued for some months until one evening when I called to collect her from her Churchtown home. There in the hallway was another suitor, Stanley Lewis. Stanley had a lot of things going for him: he and his parents were Baptists and went to the same church as Jean's, he had a car and his people had money. At this level of competition my faithful Moto Guzzi came a poor second and Jean was lost. She married Stanley and they are now living in Spain, where he owns the Aqua World water-slide complex, having sold his first business venture, Squash Ireland, to the McGrath family.

Until I met Jean I had not understood that you could feel as deeply about someone as I did about her. I also did not realise that you could be badly hurt when you were rejected. It was a lesson that I did not fully learn because, in retrospect, I think I entered into my next serious relationship a shade too quickly. The Shadows were the leading guitar group at the time and, like all budding Hank Marvins, I strutted around the bedroom imitating his swagger. I should also, perhaps, have recalled the title of their hit single "On the Rebound". It might have served my interests better.

Soon after I split up with Jean, I attended a dance in the old Longford Tennis Club in Monkstown. John Keogh and the Greenbeats were playing and I spotted a girl who wasn't dancing but was listening intently to the music. This intrigued me because, being in a band myself, I too was interested in how they presented themselves and played. We got talking and, as the old saying goes, one thing led to another. When I brought her home that night on the back of my Moto Guzzi I was struck by how fearless she was as I took corners at speed. I liked that about her and when I asked her to go out with me again Helen Gorman agreed. My friend Jimmy Dunne, whom I had brought to the dance that night as my pillion passenger, had to walk home to Seafield Drive in Booterstown.

Helen and I were both very young. She was not long out of St

Mary's Secondary School in Haddington Road, where she had excelled at her studies, and was working in the laboratory in TCD. On our first date she asked me where I had gone to school and without hesitation, remembering my scary experience with Ray Ray Farren, I replied that I had gone to Marian College. That reply seemed to satisfy her, although I am sure that the Reverend Hugh Clement was spinning in his grave at my apostasy.

But we thought we were in love and we certainly liked each other's company. Helen had an excellent singing voice and we made a good couple with me on the guitar and her on vocals. In the evenings, as Wyn and Helen, we played for pints around the town and generally enjoyed ourselves. By this time I had sold the Moto Guzzi and had invested in my first car, a second-hand Ford Escort Estate, which gave me greater mobility. The car was christened the "passion wagon" on account of the opportunity the Estate version gave to relax in comfort and have fun in the back. To emphasise its notoriety, I painted the top-half yellow and the bottom-half green. With the band of mahogany-type wood running between the colours it certainly looked the part.

In the estate agents' world, Paddy MacKeogh had just landed a major development in Sutton on Church Road. Houses on both sides of the road were to be sold. We had the sale of one side and another agent, P.J. Dwyer, had the other side. I was on commission and I set to work to sell my houses as quickly as I could. Within three weeks I had sold the entire allocation while P.J. on the other side had sold only three. From P.J.'s point of view there was only one answer to this phenomenon: he offered me a job. I was upgrading my motor portfolio pretty rapidly at this point in my life and already had a red MG Midget company car from Paddy MacKeogh. P.J. offered to buy it for me and so I was on my way again.

But I was a restless soul who, imbued with the confidence of youth, thought that I knew all there was to know about the business and that I could make a much better living working for myself. So at the age of twenty myself and another young buck, Hugh Gibney, established the firm of Beere and Gibney and rented offices in 2 Hatch Street, Dublin 2.

Now that I had my own business the sensible option, it seemed to Helen and myself, was to get married. By this time she had discovered that not only had I not attended Marian but also that I was a Protestant. We were married in St Mary's Church on Haddington Road, Dublin 4, on the 28 November 1970. My brother Ian was our best man and Ethna Traynor, Michele Smith's aunt, was our bridesmaid. The reception was held in the Montrose Hotel and the only blot on the proceedings was that my dad was not well enough to attend. We moved into a garden-level flat at Bakers Corner, near Deansgrange on the south side of Dublin, and we were very happy together. By this time Helen had transferred to the laboratory in UCD, where she was dissecting frogs legs to discover their DNA, if I remember correctly.

My dad had finally retired from the Provincial Bank in 1969 and following this my parents had decided to sell their home in Glenamena Park and move to Glasthule, just south of Dun Laoghaire, where they bought Mac's, a newsagent, tobacconist and sweet shop with accommodation over it. My brother Ian was attending a business-studies course at TCD and Graeme was at St Andrews, with both living at home.

Running the shop was difficult and was not made any easier by the discovery that, contrary to what my mother had thought, it did not have a licence to sell newspapers. If no newspapers were for sale people were less likely to come in for their cigarettes and sweets. But my mum was not to be fazed by this slight inconvenience: she just bought the papers elsewhere and sold them on at no profit. The customers came in and bought their fags and sweets and she and Dad were making a reasonable living out of Mac's.

Running any retail business is not easy. You have to be open every day, all day, and you are on your feet constantly. My dad's life-long addiction to Park Drive cigarettes and the occasional pipe was beginning to catch up with him and he was visibly slowing down. He was not able to take his walks in the hills and, in fact, it was an effort for him to get up the stairs at night. His lungs were giving out.

One day my mother was ascending a ladder while stock taking when she collapsed, fell off the steps and had to be hospitalised. It took a while for the doctors to discover what was wrong with her but they eventually decided that she had a cerebral haemorrhage and she was transferred to the Richmond Hospital. My dad, meanwhile, had been taken to St Vincent's Hospital where they had to collapse his lung to try and save his life. They could do little for him and the years of smoking Park Drive had worn out his lungs. He died in 1972 and my mum was so ill that she was unable to attend his funeral. Bonnie was interred in the Stanley family vault in Mount Jerome. Up to this point the little experience I had of funerals involved seeing a coffin being lowered into a grave. On this occasion the event was somewhat different. A great slab was removed from the top of the vault and you could see right into it. Being a curious sort of person I looked in, expecting to see a few coffins. I was taken aback to discover that I was looking at the skeletons of my ancestors lying on stone slabs. Thankfully my dad was in a coffin and I wondered had they been also and had the wood disintegrated over time. I did not like to ask. Prayers were said and we went our separate ways.

I recall visiting my mum in the Richmond Hospital at this time.

She was in a bed at the end of a long ward and I had to walk past the most harrowing sights: unfortunate people with their heads fixed to the backs of the beds so they would not be able to move and every kind of head injury you could imagine. My mother was not well and without an operation the prognosis was not good. Even with an operation we had no guarantee that she would recover. Her father, Donald, took charge of the situation and having interviewed the surgeon, a Mr Lanigan, decided that the operation was the best available option. Her head had to be shaved and the operation to seal three aneurisms in her brain was long and difficult but ultimately she pulled through. A year later she had to go through the whole procedure again but she recovered and, although she was never the same woman that she had been, she was alive.

In a very short space of time our whole family had been turned on its head and we had to find a boarding-school for Graeme because, with our father dead and our mum recovering slowly from her serious illness, home life was in turmoil. Graeme was not too happy with this but in the circumstances we had very few options available to us. Ian came up with the solution and Graeme was sent off to Sligo Grammar as a boarder. It took him a while to settle in but ultimately he made some very good friends there, many of whom he is still friendly with and some of whom work in Abrakebabra.

Our mother recovered her strength slowly but the old spark was gone. Mum was lucky to be alive but it was a cruel stroke of fate to take away so many of her faculties at such a relatively young age. Ian tried to juggle working in the shop with college but eventually had to give up the struggle. Mac's was sold and my mum and brothers moved to Ballinteer.

Beere and Gibney Ltd. were prospering and 1971 we got the sale of a large spit-level bungalow built by Joe Gormley on

Knocknacree Park in Dalkey which we sold for IR£24,000. Joe then gave us the contract to sell an estate of luxury bungalows that he had just built in Dornden Park behind the Tara Towers Hotel, where I had had that near miss with the fox all those years previously. They were priced at £15,000 each and a lot of estate agents were competing for the sale. I managed to convince Gormley to give us the agency by effectively halving the usual commission we would be expected to receive and paying for the advertising. Although this may have appeared to be a suicidal business ploy, I had a method to my apparent madness. I reckoned that as the majority of potential purchasers of the Dornden Park bungalows lived in much larger houses in the general locality they would in effect be trading down. If they were, we might very well convince them to allow us to auction their houses. The commission for auctions, at 5 per cent plus advertising paid by the purchaser, was much higher than the 2.5 per cent for private sales paid by the vendor so we thought that we could be onto a winner.

We sold all the Dornden Park bungalows in record time and we got about ten auctions from the purchasers. One of them was a large red-brick house on Park Avenue in Sandymount and this coup raised our profile in the media and earned us a lot of money.

Unfortunately, soon after this Hugh decided that with his newfound wealth he would like to emigrate to Canada to seek his fortune. I was left with the choice of either finding a new partner or shutting-up shop. I tried unsuccessfully to come up with a replacement and reluctantly decided that I did not want to continue as a sole practitioner.

With the money that I made from the Dornden Park development and its spin-offs I was able to put a deposit on my first house, 178 Broadford Avenue in Ballinteer. It was just around the corner from my mum and brothers so the Beeres were nearly back together again.

CHAPTER 8

Man of property

IT WAS 1972 and, as I was now a family man, I thought that perhaps I should see about getting a proper job with some career prospects. One day I spotted an advertisement in the paper looking for an assistant property manager with a leading commercial and industrial property company. I applied for the position and was called for interview to the MEPC Ireland Ltd offices in Fade Street, Dublin 2. MEPC stood for Metropolitan Estate Property Corporation. The managing director, Augustus Kennedy Kisch, interviewed me and for some reason we both liked each other immediately. I was short-listed and after a second interview I was offered the position with Wing Commander Squire, property manager and director, as my immediate boss.

At the time MEPC, whose headquarters were in London, was the second biggest property company in these islands and Kennedy Kisch was a major shareholder. They had built the first suburban shopping centre in Ireland in Stillorgan in 1965 for £750,000 with a low-interest loan from Friends Provident and were the dominant force in Irish property. Through their subsidiary Dublin City Properties they owned many retail and commercial freeholds in Dublin 1 and 2.

Kennedy Kisch had the facility of making whoever was in his company feel they were a most important and valued person.

1. Mount Anville House, home of Daniel Beere Attorney to the Exchequer who lived there from 1805 to 1826. The tree to the right of the house is the "Victory Tree" planted by Queen Victoria during her visit in 1853.

2. Rev. Gerald Beere MA TCD, son of Daniel Beere of Mount Anville, and my great great grandfather.

3. Raheen's Manor, Co. Clare, home of Hugh Clement Beere's mother, Thomasina Brady, my great grandmother.

4. My grandfather Rev. Hugh Clement Beere outside the Rectory at Laracor with a 1914 14hp Humber in the foreground.

5. My father Stanley, his sister Florence and his mother Eileen at Laracor Rectory in August 1929. (*below left*)

6. Stanley Beere and family at Laracor Rectory in 1926. His brother Nenon, sisters Florence and Marjorie (with dog). (*above*)

7. Rev. Hugh Clement Beere beside his Riley, June 1931. (*left*)

8. My father Stanley Beere (Bonnie), second row centre, Scoutmaster of the Donnybrook Troop, June 1932.

9. 6 hp Rover at Laracor Rectory 1924 with single cylinder, three gears, top speed 25mph. Hugh Clement sold it for £15 that year.

10. My mother Yolande Nelson (in white blouse) with the Nelson family and Rolls Royce.

11. The *Evening Herald* 12 March 1986 remembers that great St Andrews victory 1921-22 and the part that my Dad played in it. My Dad is sitting to the right of the Cup in the front row.

12. My mother Yolande on her wedding day with a corsage of orchids.

13. My father Bonnie.

14. Auntie Florence Ruttledge. (*left*)
15. My mother Yolande (Lulu) look-
    ing good. (*above*)
16. Dr Thekla Beere, who achieved
    so much. (*below left*)
17. My father at the Percy Lawn
    Tennis Club dance.

18. Me, aged two years.

19. Getting a hug from my mother Lulu.

20. Ian and I at 8 Belmont Villas with Mum.

21. At the Boy Scout Swimming
    Gala. *From left* Fletcher,
    Hamilton, Elleker, myself,
    McQuillan and White. (*above*)

22. My swimming cups and trophies
    won at the St Andrews Gala
    1962.

23. The St Andrews Junior Cup team 1962/1963 with Headmaster PJ Southgate and me third from left in the back row.

24. On a Scout trip to the Giants Causeway with the 25th Mount Merrion Troop. *From left* myself, Paddy Gorman and Dallas McCullagh.

25. Two sea bass caught by myself at Booterstown with spinning rod.

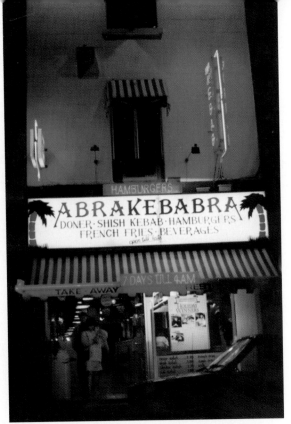

26. My Diploma for Health and Safety after completing the course in 1998.

28. The first Abrakebabra interior with the green plastic stools and green lathe ceiling. *(below)*

27. The first Abrakebabra at 11 Rathgar Road, Rathmines, where it all started. *(above)*

29. The marquee tent we used at the Féile at Thurles in August 1992. Note the twelve cash registers. (*above*)

30. The Abrakebabra "flagship" at O'Connell Bridge. (*right*)

31. The Irish cycling team, sponsored by Abrakebabra, which finished second in the 1996 Rás. (*below left*)

32. The Abrakebabra office girls: loyal and lovely. *From left* Michele, Gillian, Karen, Aileen and Sinead. (*below right*)

33. Wyn and Graeme with Angel at the opening of the 50th Abrakebabra in Kildare.

34. Graeme, Abul and Wyn in Bahrain. (*right*)

35. The plaque that marked the
opening of the first Abrakebabra in
Bahrain. (*below*)

36. The River Club, where they all hung out, featuring the Champagne Gallery and Oscar Wilde's portrait.

37. The Merchants Arch Building in Temple Bar Dublin, home to the River Club and to Abrakebabra.

38. My daughter Rosalind and I at her 21st Birthday Party in the River Club in 1998.

39. Barbeque in the Polo Club in the Phoenix Park with some friends. Liz and Conor Maguire, Shirley and I, Audrey Taylor and Des Donovan, and Tom and Aileen Morrin.

40. The Rotary Hiking Club. *From top left* Tony Keegan, Donald Gordon, Jim and Aidan Bourke, Paul Martin and me.

41. At the Abrakebabra Golf Outing in Old Conna Golf Club. *From left* Dave Kavanagh, Larry O'Mahony and Graeme.

42. At the 2004 Rotary Club of Dublin Golf Classic. *From left* Ethna Fitzgerald a Past President of the Dublin Club, Tony Keegan, President, and the principal sponsor, me.

43. At an outing in Druids Glen Golf Club with myself on the left and the Captain of Powerscourt Golf Club Chris Ball on the right. (*below*)

44. Alan Sherwood and myself at the Rotary Golf Classic. I am holding the trophy for the Champion Putter.

45. At my 50th Birthday Party. *From left* Shirley and myself, Dame Veronica Sutherland, the British Ambassador to Ireland, Charlie McCreevy, TD, Minister for Finance and his wife Noeleen and Sean Lemass.

46. The happy family, Jeff, Gavin, Wyn and Shirley.

When a discussion arose he would always ask my opinion and listen carefully until I had completed my reply. I learned a lot from him. One piece of advice I will always remember was that when dealing with a rent review, as we were constantly, you should never put the tenant to the wall, so to speak. In another five years you would be dealing with that same tenant again and, taking the long-term view, it was better that both parties should feel they did well out of the review. This was sound advice, as there is nothing as difficult to deal with as a totally dissatisfied tenant and it is sometimes not easy to put your finger on the precise reason for the dissatisfaction. He also told me that in developing a property you should always use other people's money, preferably at the lowest interest rate available.

MEPC was a fantastic company in which to work because they had built up an expertise in building, developing and letting properties and there was so much a person like me could learn about the business just by working there. I was not long with the company when one day Mr Kisch called me into his office and informed me that I was to be a chartered surveyor and that the company would pay all the fees required for me to achieve this professional qualification. Unlike other students, who attended Bolton Street during the day, I would have to study at night by correspondence course from Reading College and when and if I passed the exams, which were held in TCD, I would be given an increase in salary. My eldest son David had been born in 1973. Household expenses looked liked increasing over the next number of years. Apart from the incentive to earn more money, I recognised this offer as a great opportunity and seized it with both hands. Over the next three years I studied diligently in the evenings at home and, thanks to my hard work and the encouragement of Mr Kennedy Kisch and Wing Commander Squire, I managed to achieve first place in Ireland in my finals. This was no mean achievement when you consider that I was competing against full-time students.

While I was with MEPC the Ardilaun Centre on St Stephen's Green was to be developed and I was responsible for ensuring that over 30 people in the old tenement buildings were rehoused to their satisfaction. Collecting the rents from Laurel Hill House in Blackrock was another of my duties. This large house stood where the Blackrock Shopping Centre is now and in addition to collecting the rents each month I was given the responsibility of collecting the apples from the orchard for distribution to the management and myself. In the hall of Laurel Hill there stood a grandfather clock in which the tenants stored their milk bottles. When the house came to be demolished to make way for the shopping centre I asked Kennedy Kisch could I have the clock and he readily agreed. I restored it myself and it now stands proudly in my home, keeping perfect time.

Kennedy Kisch was a larger-than-life character and liked taking holidays in exotic locations. He and his wife often went salmon fishing in Iceland and another year he headed off to Hawaii. While there he got a cameo role in his favourite TV programme, *Hawaii Five-O*, and liked the hotel that they were staying in so much that MEPC bought it as part of their portfolio. That was his style.

Coincidentally, as well as developing the first out-of-town shopping centre MEPC also owned the first purpose-built retail centre in Dublin. This was the Dublin City Market on South Great George's Street. I was responsible for overseeing the refurbishment and design of the car-park that was destined to become a retail space. One day I had the unenviable task of explaining personally to Ben Dunne Senior that he could not park his car there any more as the space was being redeveloped into a market place. He did not take kindly to this rather inconvenient information. The basement had been used by Irish Distillers as a bonded warehouse for nearly a hundred years and when they decided to transfer their stock to Cork I was able to turn it into a much-needed underground car-park. I do not know if Ben Senior used the new facility – somehow I doubt it.

Some years after qualifying as a chartered surveyor I was asked to lecture Part Two students at Bolton Street Technical College. I enjoyed this because I have always felt that giving back something to your profession and community is an essential part of life.

In the mid-1970s, while she was living around the corner from us in Broadford Avenue in Ballinteer, my mother took in a paying guest. Ian was still at TCD and one day while looking at the college notice-board he saw a card from a maths lecturer, Jim Walker, looking for accommodation. My mother was recovering her strength slowly and we thought the extra money that a lodger would bring would be useful. Jim moved in and, like others before him, became one of the family. In fact, when Ian was married some months later Jim attended the wedding as a guest. Jim appeared to be a very successful maths lecturer and seemed to be able to trade up his cars at will.

Although my mother was a lot better, she was still a bit forgetful and at times could be a little vague. I began to notice that certain items were not where they had been. A large oak roll-top desk that had been owned by my grandfather the Reverend Hugh Clement and an Underwood typewriter had disappeared. When I asked my mother where they had gone she really hadn't a clue. Jim then told us that she had given them away to people who had called to the door. You can imagine how concerned we were at this. A woman who appeared to be getting better slowly was in fact deteriorating rapidly. We did not know what to do.

Our dilemma was solved by a visit we received from a chief

inspector from Dublin Castle who informed us that "Jim Walker" was a master forger who had altered students' passports and used them for his own purposes. All the cars that he had were stolen and when the chief inspector asked us for a photo of "Jim" for his files we discovered that the only one we had was taken at Ian's wedding. When we looked carefully at the group photograph, however, we saw that as the photographer had taken the picture "Jim" had turned his head and his face was not visible in the picture. "Jim" was wanted for embezzlement in the United Kingdom, and he was no more a maths lecturer than I was: he had just stuck the card on the board. We were all delighted that our mother had not been parting with her possessions at the front door and that her slow recovery was real.

After I had been with MEPC for some seven years Kennedy Kisch called me into his office and told me without much preamble that he had just three months to live. He went on to say that he had ensured that I would be well looked after and that in addition to MEPC shares I would be given my company car as a gift. As he foretold, three months later he was dead and things changed rapidly at the corporation.

Roger Carey from the Birmingham office was appointed Managing Director and he decided to liquidate nearly all their Irish assets. Stillorgan and Dun Laoghaire shopping centres were sold off and soon it looked as if there would be very little for me to manage. During my time with MEPC I had built up a professional relationship with Alan Bradley of Jones Lang Wootton who had carried out some valuations for us. I rang Alan and was invited to meet with John Mulcahy, a senior partner. After some discussion I was offered a position as senior surveyor and was glad to accept.

Jones Lang Wootton was a very different working environment from MEPC. At my former job I was managing property that we owned ourselves; in my new position we were managing property on behalf of a large number of clients. The staff of 70 was much bigger than I was accustomed to working with and it took me a while to become used to my new firm. I was put in charge of Donaghmede Shopping Centre, which had been owned by the Gallagher Group who were now in receivership. Laurence Crowley had been appointed as receiver and he employed Jones Lang Wootton. I was put in as property manager and my task was to prepare the property for sale. This entailed ensuring that all the units had full planning permission and there were no unauthorised developments.

I rapidly discovered that many units did not, in fact, have planning permissions and that fire corridors and other structural alterations had to be built before permissions could be obtained. At the same time dozens of rent reviews had to be dealt with, many of which went to arbitration. Because of my experience working in MEPC many, if not all, of the reviews that went to arbitration came down on my side. After a very long process the centre was ready for sale and H. Williams bought most of it. Dunnes Stores bought their own store's freehold and the protracted negotiations were conducted between Noel Fox, John and myself.

John Mulcahy, who is now managing director of Jones Lang LaSalle and is one year younger than I am, has a brilliant mind. In the ten minutes before a meeting he could read through a complicated brief and master every aspect of it. In 1979 he went to London and came back with the latest Apple computer technology, which meant we were the first property-management company to be computerised.

I also had responsibility for the Aer Lingus pension fund and up to that point had had to laboriously work out rent reviews with a calculator, paper and pen. Now at the push of a button I could increase rents by 5 per cent and immediately see what the bottom line would be. A downside of computers that I also discovered is that they can crash and you can lose all your data. This happened to me soon after we acquired the Apple and I have since learned to save diligently as I go along.

As we were also carrying out valuations for the PMPA insurance company I was sent on a writing course to the IMI to perfect my skills in this area. Valuation report writing at Jones Lang Wootton was a challenge because John demanded that the figures be exact and in the right order and Alan insisted that the language should be perfectly correct. This was great training and has stood to me in the years since.

Our second child, Ros, was born in 1977 and the following year we sold Broadford Avenue and moved to Aranleigh Vale off the Grange Road in Rathfarnham. Our family was increasing and my senior position in Jones Lang Wootton meant that I could trade up comfortably. We stayed in Aranleigh for over five years and, like all young couples, we became involved with the Residents' Association and local sports days. Helen joined the Women's Political Association (WPA).

Around 1981 I was asked by John Mulcahy to carry out a survey of the Jervis Street Hospital site in the centre of Dublin. Clients of Jones Lang Wootton had acquired the site from the hospital, which was to be transferred to Beaumont, and along with other property the idea was to develop the area as a shopping centre. I looked at the configuration of the site and decided that a central mall with retail units on each side, with a central concourse and a multi-storey car-park would be an ideal solution. The plans I had prepared were filed and I forgot about my ideas until the Jervis Centre was built incorporating many of my concepts.

One day John called me in and told me that, as I played golf, I was the right man to carry out a valuation of Baltray Golf Course. The Hartigan family owned the Baltray lands and Anne Hartigan, who had inherited the course, had requested us to value the property. Club members leased the land and as there had not been a rent review for twenty years the money paid to the Hartigans was artificially low – only £500 per annum. At the time not many golf courses were not owned by the members themselves but luckily I happened to be a member of one, Kilternan in South County Dublin, that was leased. I was easily able to discover the acreage of the course and the rent paid to the landlord. Taking into account the land values north of Drogheda and the championship nature of the course I was able to come up with a realistic valuation. Following arbitration my figure was accepted and while the members' annual subscriptions were dramatically increased the result was much fairer to all concerned.

Our third child, Jeffrey, was born in 1982 and, while Helen and I were delighted to have a second son, his arrival meant that Helen's political ambitions had to take second place to the family. In that year also my brother Graeme, who was now 24 and who had tried his hand at many different careers, began to sell kebabs out of Devaney's shop window in the south Dublin suburb of Rathmines. This simple idea of Graeme's to earn a few bob and cater for the late-night trade was to change us all and precipitate a revolution in the fast-food business in Ireland. None of our lives would ever be the same again.

CHAPTER 9

A slice of magic

T HE HUMBLE KEBAB, which was to cause a revolution in Ireland's fast-food market, originated in Turkey. It is one of Europe's most ancient dishes and a well-cooked kebab provides a unique and subtle combination of lamb, spices and herbs. With the migration of Turkish workers to Germany in the 1960s the kebab began to become more readily available in Western Europe. It was generally believed at the time that Irish people preferred bland meat and two veg and the only fast-food available was fish and chips and burgers. However, in England there was evidence of more exploratory cuisine and small late-night kebab shops began to open in London and other English cities.

I remember, during a trip to London, seeing kebabs being sold from a small shop off Piccadilly Circus and, although I did not know it at the time, Tony Hannigan, a friend of Graeme's, was selling kebabs in Merrion Row in Dublin. He had a small shop, it was not well known and it was dark and dingy. Another problem Tony had was that the Irish flour that he was using to make the pitta bread was not suitable and the kebabs easily fell apart. When our time came we got around this by importing the pitta bread from London, through Tony.

The doner kebab is the basis for the kebab as the customer knows it. It consists of minced lamb, combined with a selection of herbs and spices, which is then pressed into the distinctive conical shape using a specially constructed broiler. At this point it is also given a binding agent, usually fat and egg, before being roasted on a spit. A doner is usually ten or twenty pounds in weight and when carved it produces a long wafer-thin strip of meat that you could call "a slice of magic". A number of these slices are then stuffed into pitta bread and topped with salads and sauces.

One of our early employees, Djillali Sai, who later became one of our first franchisees in Blanchardstown, managed to make a doner weighing 40 pounds and he later told me that his arms used to hang off. He was so proud of the achievement that he wouldn't tell us how exhausted he was.

In the early 1980s Graeme was trying to run a fleet of trucks but because of continual breakdowns it was turning out to be extremely hard work for limited financial return. Graeme had also sold burgers out of the back of one of his vans when the Pope came to Ireland in 1979. In 1982 he was living with his wife Margaret in a flat over Devaney's off-licence in Rathmines. He began to sell kebabs out of a window in the shop below on weekends to make a few bob.

Rathmines was teeming with students and young people who lived in the thousands of flats that dotted it and the surrounding areas. The flats and bed-sits had little or no cooking facilities and the tenants had about the same level of interest in catering for themselves. After a few pints of an evening, how better to keep the calorie level up than a visit to a handy fast-food emporium? The problem was, apart from the ubiquitous fish-and-chip shop, there was nowhere to go.

There are many versions of how Abrakebabra started but it is an unequivocal fact that Graeme Beere opened the first restaurant in Rathmines, Dublin 6, in December 1982. My version of events is that our aunt Patricia Rutledge died and my two brothers and myself inherited £9,000 between us. This was exactly the amount that our father, Bonnie, ought to have received upon his own father's, the Reverend Hugh Clement Beere's, death in the 1950s. My father's sister, remembering her brother's disinheritance, redressed the wrong perpetrated all those years ago in this gesture towards her three nephews.

My middle brother, Ian, being a more conservative and risk-adverse schoolteacher, put his money into an extension to his house. Graeme and I had the seed capital for entrepreneurial activity.

The idea of selling fast food to younger customers was my brother Graeme's brainchild. He came to me with the idea and, not only did I tell him that I thought it had potential, I also loaned him the £3,000 I had inherited from my aunt. As far as I can recall, Graeme's friend Dony McDonald came up with the name Abrakebabra based on "abracadabra", the magical password used in the *Arabian Nights*, with the word "kebab" cleverly inserted in the middle. The Steve Millar song "Abracadabra" had been a huge hit some months previously and put the word into our heads. The entire concept of the name and the selling of the kebab were born with "Abrakebabra – fast food, magic service". I did have some doubts about the name at the time. I remember thinking that it was possibly too long, that people might not understand it and that they would not catch on to the word play. Thankfully, I was proved wrong. People still have fun trying to pronounce Abracadabra or Abrakebabra and they still get it wrong sometimes. Most of the staff and our families affectionately refer to the company as simply "Abra".

The distinctive logo comprising the word "Abrakebabra" shaded by two lush palm trees was designed by Dony and

Graeme and was very clever and a great hit with the punters.

Wearing my property hat I went looking for a site in the Rathmines area. As luck would have it James McKee, who worked with me in Jones Lang Wootton, had had a dry-cleaning business at 11 Rathgar Road, opposite the Garda station. There had been a fire and he was trying to part with the lease for no premium with a rent of £10,000 p.a. Graeme and I went to see it and we were both excited at its potential. My knowledge of the property world was a key factor at this stage. Planning permission in 1982 was much easier to acquire than it is today but nevertheless required a professional approach. We obtained permission for take-away business use because in those days, as it had had a retail use, the planners agreed that a fast-food business was retail also.

The fit-out for Rathmines cost about £10,000. I can remember the slabs going down – concrete garden slabs, 2 foot by 2 foot, for £1 each. The ceiling was sprayed black and a timber lattice sprayed green hid the fire damage above.

Graeme ran the shop and I came in after work and at weekends. We offered very good fresh food at a competitive price and served with a smile. Pitta bread is unleavened and the traditional meat filling in each kebab is a third of a pound of lamb. After a few years we needed to kill 500 sheep a week to supply our shops. There were three sauces – chilli, mayonnaise and garlic – and we learned how to prepare the food from an expert kebab chef, whom we met in London. We insisted on using the best quality lettuce and the freshest red and green sweet peppers.

Our concept was based on the McDonald's shop in Grafton Street, which we later learned had a greater turnover than its US counterparts. We incorporated their idea of a clean, bright and trendy restaurant with both the floor and walls tiled. I can still see in my mind's eye the small, green, plastic stools with no back to them. Later we moved on to the McDonald's version, with a very hard bucket-type seat.

Staff wages were £2.50 per hour. This was a very good rate for the time and there was no difficulty in hiring: people would just walk in, look for a job and maybe start the same night, helping the chef who was making the kebabs and putting them up on the front two skewers. The menu was pretty basic, consisting of kebabs, burgers and chips. At the beginning kebabs cost £1 and they stayed at that price for years.

Ireland in 1982 was not a very promising place in which to start a new business. Not only was the Celtic Tiger asleep, he was not even imagined by the economists. In 1977 the new Fianna Fáil government had proposed the abolition of domestic rates and car tax in their election manifesto. Unsurprisingly they won by a massive majority. An international oil crisis intervened and the intended boost to the economy, by giving people more money to spend, never materialised. Five years later, we were in the middle of a deep depression. National borrowing rose, as did emigration and unemployment levels.

But when you are young and blessed with optimism, thoughts of failure never enter your head. Graeme had very little to lose and after a couple of weeks the Rathmines restaurant was turning over £3–4,000 a week. With a rent of £10,000 a year and fit-out costs of £10,000 it was a licence to print money. Suddenly Graeme had so much money he did not know what to do with it.

CHAPTER 10

The road to riches

BOUT A YEAR after opening in Rathmines we decided to open a second restaurant. This was not a difficult decision to make and was testimony to the phenomenal success of our first venture into the exotic world of the kebab. Ireland was so ready and willing to sample these eastern delights that it seemed a pity to confine our efforts to just one locality. There was also the small fact that Abrakebabra seemed to be a very lucrative venture. We decided to go again.

Graeme paid back the loan that I had given him to start up in Rathmines and I, in turn, used that money, along with more from the now cash-rich Graeme, to start a second shop with a bank loan from Guinness and Mahon.

The second shop was destined to be 3 Upper Baggot Street, near the bridge over the canal. I had identified the area as a suitable location for an Abrakebabra shop as it had all the necessary ingredients for success: flats, young people, pubs and little or no competition. The only difference was that it was a bit more up-market than Rathmines.

I walked up and down Baggot Street, calling into each shop, until I found a Mr O'Connor who had a sub-post office with a newsagent's business attached and who had decided to retire. From my experience in the property business I knew that the rent that he was asking, £10,000 a year, was reasonable and we signed for the lease there and then on the back of an envelope. The contract read, "I agree to let Mr Beere my premises for £10,000 per year." He later tried to renegotiate our agreement because the pub on the corner had offered him £15,000, but I had his signature and was paying what he had asked. I had also agreed that I would be responsible for obtaining planning permission and I had written that into the agreement. The contract stood and we had our second shop.

Although the Baggot Street outlet was slightly smaller than Rathmines, it was perhaps a sign of our increased wealth that the fit-out cost around £30,000 compared to the £10,000 of the original restaurant.

Baggot Street was another success story. The punters rolled in, thousands of kebabs, burgers and chips were consumed and I began to really question what I should be doing with my time. I had put a manager into Baggot Street and was holding down a job with Jones Lang Wootton.

The recession had hit the property business pretty hard and Jones Lang Wootton were in the process of reducing their staff from 70 to about 50. Many of the surveyors went to London to find work but, with my family in Dublin and the restaurant in Baggot Street, this was never really an option for me. I worked hard carrying out valuations and rent reviews during the day and in the evenings I worked in the restaurant.

There are, however, only so many hours in the day and it was very obvious that an investment of my time in Abrakebabra would reap greater rewards than in the rather more respectable world of property. So I opted to leave Jones Lang Wootton for the more lucrative and exciting fast-food life. It made absolute sense that I should spend my time where my money was.

Abrakebabra Ltd was registered with Graeme and I each holding 50 per cent of the share capital. The partnership that was formed was destined to last for eighteen years and would bring elation, heartbreak, riches and lots of fun – not necessarily in that order.

Our third restaurant was opened at O'Connell Bridge, in the Ballast House on the corner of Westmoreland Street and Aston Quay, in December 1984. At 1,500 square feet, it was our largest outlet so far and for the first time we were moving right into the centre of Dublin city. The premises had been owned by Carousel Travel who had gone into liquidation and John McNally, with whom I had studied auctioneering, was selling it for the liquidator, Mr Pomeroy. It was withdrawn at auction and, having paid the liquidator's fees of £2,000, we took over the lease for a premium of £24,000 with a rent of £30,000 p.a.

O'Connell Bridge had three floors: 800 square feet in the basement, which was the main seating area, 400 square feet on the ground floor and 300 square feet on the mezzanine. To satisfy the planning authorities that no food odours would emanate from our premises onto the street, and because we had no back entrance, we invested in a state-of-the-art air change unit. Designed by an architect friend of mine, Dave Gilligan, it consisted of a bank of nylon and charcoal filters above the cooking area. The equipment was the equivalent of having a turbo jet in the building and the vibrations were so great that we had to replace the tiles several times. The unit passed the fumes from our cooking operation through three sets of filters before they hit the street completely odour free.

Because of its size and the necessity for a custom-built air change unit, the fit-out costs of O'Connell Bridge were a multiple of the Baggot Street costs. At this stage our bankers, Ulster Bank, got cold feet and would not back us. We went to

Christy Hayes, who was manager of the O'Connell Street branch of the Bank of Ireland. Christy listened to our story, inspected the figures and told us we could have the money that we wanted if we moved all our business to his branch. We agreed to this and he loaned us the money we required.

I remember sitting by myself in the basement of the O'Connell Bridge restaurant soon after we had opened. There were no customers and I was thinking that I had made a great mistake regarding my career change. A week later my misgivings were proved to be unfounded and we had a turnover of £3,000 a week and growing.

The opening of the O'Connell Bridge restaurant right in the heart of our capital city had a major impact in raising brand awareness of the Abrakebabra name among the general public. There were a large number of pubs and clubs in the vicinity and there was an immense passing trade. Because we were situated in such a prime central location we were often used as a backdrop on many national TV programmes showing scenes of central Dublin, including the Saint Patrick's Day parade.

It was one of my biggest coups to obtain that location so near to O'Connell Bridge. In my opinion, and judging by turnover figures, it is the best site in Ireland for a fast-food restaurant. It is visible from any number of directions: from O'Connell Street, the quays, the bridge itself and from Westmoreland Street. It is a prime location in the very heart of the capital. Soon after we opened, turnover soared to £10,000 per week, which was enormous. The O'Connell Bridge restaurant has always been one of the most successful in the Abrakebabra chain.

But there was one problem with O'Connell Bridge that we had not foreseen: as it operated on three levels, customers, who from time to time could be either tired, drunk, emotional or all three, had to negotiate flights of stairs that they could slip on if the steps became wet. To try to resolve the problem we decided to employ a cleaning lady that would do nothing else but clean the stairs and ensure that they were completely dry. Unfortunately, she slipped herself and ended up claiming against us. The irony of the situation was not lost on us. We immediately laid a non-slip floor, improved the lighting on the stairwell and installed cameras so we could verify if an accident was genuine. You learn as you go along.

I then looked around the south side of Dublin to identify a suitable location for our fourth restaurant. Donnybrook was well known to us, as we had lived off Belmont Avenue. Although we had moved about two miles out the Stillorgan Road, we still socialised in the area and knew how hard it was to obtain any food for ourselves after the pubs closed. The O'Reilly-Hyland family owned 3 Donnybrook Mall and, as luck would have it, I had worked with their son Charlie O'Reilly-Hyland in Jones Lang Wootton. My background in the property business was, once again, an asset. Number 3 had operated as a Chinese take-away and as no rent had been paid for a considerable time the landlords were anxious to put more reliable tenants in.

There was no question of us taking over the Chinese take-away's lease. They were gone, the locks were changed and Alsatian dogs had been put in to discourage their return. So we had to agree to a brand-new lease. What we did not know was that the landlord had increased the rent to us from £10,000 to £14,000 per annum. The other tenants in the mall were due a rent review in a couple of months. So when a comparison was made between the existing rents and ours the other tenants also had their rents raised. We also discovered that although the Chinese business had operated as a take-away, and even said so on the sign over the shop front, they had only had planning permission for a restaurant. The planning authorities wanted to close us down and for a year after we opened we had to have a sign in our restaurant that read "No take-aways allowed". After a lot of hassle we managed to persuade the authorities that we were providing a much-needed service, that in reality there was no change of use and that we would be a great asset to the neighbourhood. They agreed.

Our troubles in Donnybrook were not completely over, however. Some years later a woman fell from the top of the stairs and she sued us. She employed an engineer to measure each step and it transpired that the risers were not of equal height. That cost us £30,000 in damages. The previous tenants had installed the stairs without much regard to uniformity and we had unwittingly inherited a complete nightmare. We immediately checked all the stairs in the other branches to see if their risers were of equal height and discovered that those in O'Connell Bridge were unequal. The stairs were rebuilt and the problem solved without any further accidents occurring. Experience can't be readily bought, as we learned to our cost.

At this time everything was run on a small scale. I was in charge of the property and financial side of the business while Graeme dealt with staff and the operational running of the restaurants. We shared an office over the Rathmines shop and saw each other every day. As the shops did not open until noon, we did not have to be at our desks until about 10.30 a.m., which meant that we missed the rush hour completely, although it was, of course, necessary to work late into the evening. Our desks were at either end of a boardroom-style table and we were constantly reacting, addressing the flow of problems that arises from a business with a large number of employees working shifts and dealing with the public. As we were working so close to each other it was easy to chat and to reach decisions quickly – even when one or other of us was talking on the phone, as was often the case. We oversaw the hiring of all staff and in the early days we managed to employ two excellent and trustworthy people who, having proved themselves, became our first Abrakebabra restaurant managers.

In a very short space of time I had moved from being an employee of a leading firm of estate agents, earning £15,000 a year and having little or no prospects, to being a 50 per cent partner in a thriving business, earning nearly twice that. It was a very exciting and financially rewarding time for my family and myself.

CHAPTER 11

Magic by design

ALTHOUGH WE HAD taken our original design ideas, as much else, from McDonald's in Grafton Street – their flagship operation in Ireland, which incorporated all the latest ideas to maximise sales and keep the customers coming back for more – there were also differences between the two operations. These differences were mostly in the range of duties undertaken by staff, which were more varied in Abrakebabra, and in the fact that we found a niche market for ourselves by remaining open until 4.30 a.m. McDonald's and other similar outlets closed at midnight.

The design package that Graeme, Dony McDonald and myself came up with for the first restaurant in Rathmines has evolved over the years and been adapted to suit different locations. But the basic, simple-but-striking green, white and red Abrakebabra logo has been a constant. Flanked by two slightly tipsy palm trees it now glows over 55 restaurants throughout Ireland. About five years ago we peaked with 65 restaurants. Red was for vibrancy and immediacy, white indicated cleanliness and green was intended to evoke an Irish and patriotic feeling. The overall intention was that the logo represented something eye-catching and exotic.

Mirroring the Abrakebabra logo, the restaurant's colour scheme reproduced the green, white and red theme, from staff uniforms to seating. Thus the seats were green, the supporting table poles red and the tables themselves white.

An Abrakebabra restaurant layout is the same in Dublin as it is in Cork or Galway, the only concessions being to the actual dimensions of the premises. The average restaurant size is around 1,200 square feet. As you approach an Abrakebabra restaurant the first thing that strikes you, apart from the distinctive logo, is the kebab freshly roasting on a skewer in the window. As you enter, the long, sleek rectangular counter is usually on your right and the bright logo is again emblazoned across its front. The counter is ideally 22 feet long by 7 feet wide (including the food-preparation area). The floors and walls are tiled for easy cleaning and to give a sharp, modern look. Toilets are located to the rear. The floor tiles are slightly ribbed to give a better grip and to inhibit slipping, which is extremely important, as we had learned.

Behind and above the counter the menu is plainly on view and the staff are waiting to take your order from noon to 4 a.m. Bright lighting and loud music add to the trendy atmosphere, as does the modern art that adorns the walls. Walking into an Abrakebabra restaurant was, and is, meant to be a unique experience – a place that was Irish yet exotic, a place to be seen.

The behind-the-counter design is impressive, visually and functionally. Unlike a staff member in a McDonald's restaurant, an Abrakebabra employee must be able to carry out all cooking and serving tasks. The serving area is designed for this specific purpose. Every utensil and cooking appliance must be easily accessible and the layout of each piece of equipment is designed with this in mind. Each staff member must be able to manoeuvre easily in this compact space.

The heavy-duty cooking appliances run along the back section of the service area. There are also a series of extractor fans along this wall to ensure adequate ventilation. From left to right there are large food lamps, where the freshly prepared food is placed as it is made so it can be served piping hot to the customer. Next is the burger grill and beside this is the deep fat fryer. On the extreme right is the kebab skewer, the anchor product, slowly rotating, being cooked evenly by a large gas cooker.

To educate the Irish public on eating such a new type of food we came up with the idea of putting a series of cartoons in each shop, showing how to eat a kebab. We had a large, jolly-looking fellow holding his kebab wrapped, as we would normally do it. In the next picture he was shown unfolding his wrapped kebab and placing the wrapping paper down flat, laying the narrow end of the kebab over the top of the wrapping and containing the majority of the kebab lying horizontally within the paper. Next the cartoon showed how to quickly fold the two sides of the wrapping around the kebab. Finally it was ready for consumption, clean, easy and mess free – well, almost. To help the customer further we provided little sachets with foil-packed lemon-scented cloths, like those you get on an aeroplane. These, being slightly dampened, were more successful than a napkin.

To the front of the counter is the food-preparation area. Staff members are trained to face front when preparing food, enabling the customer to witness the production process first hand. On the far right there is a pitta bread toaster; beside this is a section where large stainless-steel vats keep the freshly sliced kebab meat and selected sauces hot. If a customer has ordered a kebab, they can watch as their toasted pitta bread is filled with slices of lamb, then with helpings of cabbage, salad and peppers and finally the three sauces – chilli, garlic and mayonnaise. To the extreme left of the counter is the till. This positioning serves a number of practical purposes. First, it facilitates the orderly queuing of customers – at peak times the queue can extend out of the door onto the street. Second, while customers are waiting they can observe the activity behind the counter and be reassured and entertained by what they see. If they are eating-in, the customers then carry their trays to the seating area.

In the early days Abrakebabra had little black plastic stools, which we later changed to bucket-type stools. These were specifically designed to encourage the customer to eat quickly and leave. In more recent years we have introduced bench seating, which is more comfortable and hopefully encourages the customer to stay longer and eat and drink more. The latest idea is the café look, with chrome seating and tables. Having eaten, the customer is encouraged to dispose of the biodegradable packaging and waste in large, well-displayed bins located around the store.

Our packaging was not always biodegradable but my long-standing interest in all aspects of nature encouraged me to try to find a product that our customers could use easily and that could be disposed of in an eco-friendly fashion. With my encouragement, Julian Money of RAP developed a beeswax-coated paper that dissolved in water and could be used to hold burgers, chips and kebabs. Pat Kenny of RTÉ fame launched this packaging line in the Shelbourne Hotel and we have a lovely picture of Pat, with model Caroline Morahan, now of *Off the Rails* fame and us with the new packaging.

Abrakebabra's prices were competitive compared to traditional take-away outlets but with us, customers had the additional option of eating their food in a warm, trendy and fun environment. We anticipated that there would be peaks and troughs in trading during the sixteen-hour day we were open for business. Off-peak hours were usually during the afternoon, while peak hours were from 11 p.m. to 2 a.m. The two shifts were from noon to 8 p.m. and 8 p.m. to 4.30 a.m.

The core product is the doner kebab and the blend of herbs and spices was fine-tuned to suit the Irish palate. Alongside the kebab are the universally popular burgers and French fries. The menu was deliberately kept simple and it was not until the 1990s that we expanded our product range from 5 to 35 to keep abreast of changing Irish tastes. However, even today the kebab remains one of the top sellers, accounting for 27 per cent of overall product sales.

As I have mentioned, when we opened the first shop our kebabs were made largely by hand before being compressed in a broiler. Although this was an excellent, tried-and-trusted method it did not lend itself to mass production. As the number of shops grew we looked around for a more efficient way of making kebabs and found that none existed.

Around the same time we discovered that, as we required upwards of 500 sheep a week to be killed, each shop needed to have its own cold-storage facility. Such a facility would insulate us, to some extent, from the vagaries of the sheep market that could see huge variations in price that we could not pass on to our customers.

To deal with both these problems we designed kebab-making equipment that consisted of three stainless-steel buckets with holes in them. A pneumatic ram activated by two red buttons four feet apart, which required the use of both hands for safety purposes, squeezed down on the lamb mince, mixed with herbs and spices and a binding agent. As it pressed down any water and air was extruded through the holes and you ended up with a perfectly formed kebab.

Working with patent agent Frank Gorman we successfully applied for a patent, which meant that we were entitled to a 10 per cent royalty on all our kebab sales. As patent income is tax-free, this came in very handy later on. We were also able to manufacture large numbers of kebabs when the price of sheep was in our favour and store them for up to six months, thus avoiding market peaks. Jack and Vinney Massey were our kebab-meat suppliers and Vinney is still providing the succulent lamb for all Abrakebabra restaurants; Jack, a former chairman of the Irish Nationwide Building Society, passed away a few years ago. I always found him to be a gentleman.

We imported our chips from Lamb and Weston in Holland where, due to the alluvial soil, the potatoes had less sugar content than in Ireland and were of a more consistent quality. Their factory extended over twenty acres and, having been peeled and cleaned, the potatoes were taken by a conveyor belt and shot at speed through a honeycomb blade that produced perfectly formed chips. They were then dry frozen and stored at the Allied Foods facility in Cork from where they could be delivered by freezer trucks to the restaurants as demand dictated.

Lettuce and peppers were bought fresh from the local market and our sauces were obtained from Rich Sauces in Belfast. We were one of their early customers and they now supply sauces throughout Europe. Our burgers came from Jim Lucey of Rangeland, County Monaghan, and in the competitive world of Irish fast food we always contended that they were thicker than McDonald's. Jim's factory was the most modern in these islands and had very effective metal detection, which ensured that the burgers we sold were succulent and safe to eat.

Our soft-drinks suppliers were Pepsi, who gave hello money of £10,000 for each new restaurant. "Hello money" is a promotional incentive sometimes provided by suppliers to customers when a new outlet is opened to encourage them to continue with the existing relationship. In our case, the money paid for the neon signage. As each customer bought a soft drink with their meal, Pepsi's sales figures for each shop were invaluable. We were able to compare them to food product sales and detect any divergence. Even with soft-drink sales there were scams. As each canister appeared to be the same when full and when empty, they were all weighed both entering and leaving the restaurant. This removed the temptation so that a full canister could not be removed and carried out as though it was empty.

However, it was early days for us: we had yet to learn the hard lessons that business often teaches.

CHAPTER 12

First franchise

B Y 1985 OUR FOUR restaurants in Rathmines, Upper Baggot Street, O'Connell Bridge and Donnybrook were attracting customers from noon to 4 a.m. very successfully. Difficulties were becoming apparent, however, that we had not foreseen. Graeme and I were the managers and we could only devote so much time to each shop. Cash was pouring in and much physical effort was required to count it and transport it to the bank, never mind the worry that cash might go missing in other ways. In a cash business there are many opportunities to siphon-off money. After being in business for three years we thought we knew all the pitfalls but, as we were to discover, we did not know the half of them.

At the same time we knew that there was a demand for our product throughout Dublin and we thought throughout the whole of Ireland. If we did not satisfy that demand, the odds were that someone else with a similar product would. This was the dilemma that faced us. Management time was limited and it would take a considerable effort and an astute investment in people to bring on a layer of senior management that we could trust. There were no easy answers and we were too caught up with keeping track of the four existing restaurants to even begin to ask the questions. The money was rolling in and it was a constant task to keep track of everything that a thriving business required.

The answer to the problem came from an unlikely source. We were approached by a man named Cheriff, a French Algerian who was married to an Irish girl and was the manager of Pat Grace's Famous Fried Chicken restaurant in Crumlin Shopping Centre – a clone of Colonel Sanders' Kentucky Fried Chicken. Over a period of time Cheriff had saved some money and wanted to go out on his own. He had seen the great success of Abrakebabra and wished to be a part of it. However he did not want to be a manager: he wanted to own his own restaurant and use our name. He wanted to be a franchisee.

Graeme and I talked it over and decided that, taking into account the difficulties outlined above and the fact that he had a proven record of good management in the fast-food business, we would progress the matter further.

A good location was, I felt, the most important factor in the setting-up of a new restaurant so I drove out to Crumlin to talk to Cheriff and to have a look around for a good site. Unbelievably, there was a shop right beside where he worked with a "For sale" sign in its window. It was an uncanny coincidence and too good an opportunity to be missed. Cheriff handed in his notice and took over the lease. While the new restaurant was being fitted-out he worked in Abrakebabra and learned how we did things.

Our knowledge of franchising at the time was very limited and when our solicitor advised us that a term of three years was the proper time for an agreement we concurred. We set the fee at 9 per cent of turnover and in early 1986 the restaurant opened. Cheriff was a lovely guy and an extremely hard worker and made a great success of Crumlin. He was also a very astute businessman and when the franchise lease came up for renewal in 1988 he effectively had us over a barrel when he demanded a reduction in our percentage take to 6 per cent (net of VAT). After a lot of negotiation we settled on 6 per cent plus 1 per cent for advertising: these figures remain, today, the norm in our business. Cheriff now has two Eddie Rockets' and five Abrakebabras – in Phibsboro, Finglas, Portmarnock and Westmoreland Street in addition to Crumlin – and is just one of the many people who, working hard and long hours, have made a very successful career from Abrakebabra.

Many of our franchisees are French Algerian and Cheriff acted as a kind of unofficial ambassador between us and his fellow-countrymen, who in turn respected him. He is a very wise man and uniquely had our confidence and their confidence at the same time.

In a cash business like Abrakebabra you are always going to attract the attention of the criminal fraternity and one day Cheriff found himself in a very dangerous situation from which he was lucky to escape with his life.

At the time, he owned Abrakebabra restaurants in Crumlin, Phibsboro and Leixlip and had worked out a routine for collecting cash from both. Unfortunately for Cheriff he was being watched and a criminal was aware of his schedule also. One day, in the car-park behind the Leixlip restaurant, he had about £12,000 in cash on his person and in his car. A man approached him wielding a gun and demanded that he hand over the cash immediately. Cheriff pushed him aside and tried to get into his car to make his getaway. He did not know another armed criminal was behind him. This one fired three shots into Cheriff and badly injured him. The criminals took the money and Cheriff was rushed to hospital where he was operated on and two bullets were removed. They were unable to remove the third, which, I believe, is still lodged in his body. He is some man.

Around the time that Cheriff was opening the first franchised Abrakebabra in Crumlin, we decided to open a company-owned restaurant in Galway. Notwithstanding all the pressures on management, we were not fully convinced that franchising was the way forward. We decided on Galway because it was, in effect, the youth capital of Ireland. It was a thriving and vibrant city with a large proportion of its population under the age of 30. The presence of University College Galway was a major factor in the area. It was a bustling, lively place and the word was there was great "craic" to be had.

The Galway company restaurant was one of our few failures and an analysis of why it failed is instructive, although it was time consuming and annoying. We found a site on Eglinton Street, which is quite close to the centre of the city. It was not a great site to begin with. We had to build a dividing wall 90 feet long by 40 feet high to bisect two buildings. The fit-out was a nightmare in that the counter had to run across the back of the premises, like McDonald's, and the customer had to walk the full 90 feet to get to it. From this we discovered that the way the counters were sited in our existing shops, to the right as you walk in, was by far the best way to attract customers.

Every second weekend I drove down to Galway with my youngest son, Jeffrey, in the back of my Mercedes 380SL. I enjoyed the drive because now that I was able to afford the cars I had always wanted I relished the opportunity to drive them. Eglinton Street, however, was not the best street and the turnover compared to our other restaurants wasn't great. After a couple of years we sold on the shop and set about acquiring a site on the corner of Eyre Square.

Here we ran into further difficulties, in that the landlord, Irish Life, did not want to transfer the lease to us from the Benetton franchisee that had previously operated there. We had taken an assignment of the lease, were trading for three years and Irish Life would just not give consent. In fact, it turned out that they wanted this prime site for themselves. We had embarked on the legal route when I invited David Went, the new CEO of Irish Life, to lunch in Peacock Alley. We had been at The High School and actually played together on the first XV. Over lunch he had to agree that Irish Life could not unreasonably withhold consent to the transfer. A week later everything was sorted out, the lease was transferred and three-years' back rent was paid over. My knowledge of property law and my contacts had won the day again. The Eyre Square restaurant was franchised out and proved to be one of our best outlets with an excellent turnover and the site gave us great visibility in the city.

Soft drinks are an integral part of any fast-food business. Although we had often played off our soft-drinks suppliers against one another when we had dealt in cans, when we moved over to canisters we decided that we would go with Pepsi. They offered us the best deal and, anyhow, Coca-Cola were in McDonald's – although we had copied much of their operation we also wanted to be seen as a separate and distinct experience. Around 1988, however, Coca-Cola, who had continued to try to obtain the soft-drinks concession in our restaurants, invited Graeme and me on a nine-day trip to the US. It is not often that a nine-day trip can change your life but in our case it certainly did.

Our first stop was New York. I went to bed quite early after the long flight but Graeme had arranged to meet a friend and both of them went out on the town. We had an early morning meeting so I was up at eight and met Graeme returning from his night out. I made the meeting and he was in recovery mode for most of the day. Our next stop was Boston where we met an architect who showed us around the city. There was a wonderful location for a restaurant in the Harvard Square area that was currently occupied by Petit Bon Pain. We seriously considered taking on the lease but decided against it because we were expanding so fast in Ireland we could hardly keep up with the business there, never mind in the US. However, we did manage to meet the lawyers and to register our name in New York, where it is still registered.

When we got to Atlanta a stretch limo was put at our disposal by Coca-Cola for the duration of our stay in the city. We were taken to the Cheetah Club, a tabletop-dancing bar the likes of which I had never seen before. We then went to the Coca-Cola head office, which is in itself an amazing building, where we were given the full tour and treated to a history of the company. The associate director who was wining and dining us told us about the concept of selling a soft drink with every order and meal. He told us that our staff should always ask the customer if they would like a soft drink with their order, with a smile. We introduced this immediately on our return to Ireland and, as well as proving an excellent money-spinner, it was, as I have already noted, a good check on the amount of food sales that a restaurant should have. Through supplying McDonald's, Coca-Cola were well aware of the importance of maximising sales.

When we got back from the US the Coca-Cola distributor in Ireland contacted us and they quoted us a price far in excess of what we were getting from Pepsi. So we decided to stay with our existing supplier.

The major benefit of our trip to the States was the information that we gleaned from Coca-Cola executives on the McDonald's operation throughout the world. At that time McDonald's had upwards of 10,000 stores worldwide and, while we were "small potatoes", we still had similar problems to solve and similar opportunities to maximise profits. We learned in Atlanta how franchising really works, what a contract that is fair to both sides should contain and that three years is a ridiculously short time to tie someone into a franchising agreement.

We came back with a very clear vision of how our business should be expanded and immediately set about finding the right kind of people to bring our plans to fruition. For us the signposts to success were very clear and we were determined to bring the joy of eating kebabs to the four corners of Ireland and beyond.

CHAPTER 13

Franchising:
the magic formula

O N M Y R E T U R N to Ireland I immediately set about filling in the gaps, and they were pretty big, in my knowledge of franchising. We had been given so much information in such a short space of time in Atlanta that it was difficult to process everything we had heard and see how it could be applied to our own operation. What I learned about franchising was fascinating. It was much more widespread than I had thought and its roots go right back into history. I also was given a present, by Michael Mehigan the owner of the McDonald's Dublin franchise, of Ray Krock's book *Churning it Out*.

The beginnings of franchising can be traced to eighteenth-century Britain, where the brewery's tied houses were an early form. Tied houses could only sell the products of the particular brewery to which they were "tied". This is still the case in many parts of Britain. But it is to the US, the home of modern franchising, that we must look to fully appreciate what can be achieved with this business model.

Isaac Singer did a lot more than invent the Singer sewing-machine: he is also credited with inventing modern franchising, which he perceived to be a necessity in the expansion of his business. When Singer began to sell his machines he discovered that before anyone would buy them they needed to be taught how to use them. Singer's solution to this problem was to sell the rights to the marketing of Singer sewing-machines to local business people, who would in turn train the purchasers to use them. Using this method of rapid expansion Singer was able to virtually corner the sewing-machine market throughout the world. To this day Singer is still one of the leading brands.

Franchising is defined as an arrangement in which "the owner of a protected trademark grants to another person or firm … the right to operate under this trademark for the purpose of producing or distributing a product or service". There are two types of franchising agreements: product franchising and business format franchising. With product franchising, "a supplier franchises (authorises) retailers to be a part of its system of selective or exclusive distribution". The focus with product franchising is on what is sold.

Business format franchising refers to an "entire business format in which one firm (the franchiser) licenses a number of outlets (franchisees) to market a product or service". These franchisees then engage in a business already developed by the franchiser using the latter's trade names, trademarks, service marks, know-how and methods of doing business. In return the franchisee pays royalties and fees to the franchiser. The franchisee usually agrees to adhere to the requirements of the franchiser regarding product mix, operating procedures and quality standards. In return the franchiser typically agrees to provide managerial, advertising and marketing assistance, training, standard operating procedures and site selection. Most of the growth in franchising in recent years has come from business format franchising.

For many companies, franchising is an efficient way to consider expanding a business. It enables a franchiser to avail of the capital and other resources available to a franchisee and it means that a franchiser can focus its efforts on growing the franchise business and improving the brand further, rather than being involved in the day-to-day management of an operation. Also, the greater the number of members of a franchise network the greater the franchiser's central purchasing power becomes.

For others, franchising is an attractive way to consider starting in business on their own account. Training and ongoing support can be accessed from the franchiser. You are also immediately part of a well-established and well-known business. You will probably be able to generate profits earlier and it is proven that you will be less likely to fail than if you were starting a new business from scratch.

The franchise way of doing business has grown in popularity over the past 25 years and nowadays some of the biggest brand-names globally are run on a franchise basis, including Benetton, Burger King, McDonald's, Domino's Pizza and Snap Printing. The most successful Irish franchise operations are Abrakebabra, O'Brien's Irish Sandwich Bars and Eddie Rocket's. The phenomenon of franchising is here to stay and represents a powerful and successful form of business in the Irish economy, with an estimated turnover of around £1.5 billion per annum.

In the late 1980s, however, franchising was a relatively new phenomenon and Graeme and I had a lot to learn. One of the first lessons was that the franchise contract should be for a period of ten years and not the three-year period that we had set for our first franchisee in Crumlin. We also learned that the sign hanging over the franchisee's restaurant should remain our property and should be paid for by us initially. Our agreement with our soft-drinks supplier, Pepsi, proved very useful in this regard in that the £10,000 hello money that they provided to us for each new outlet could be used exclusively for signage that remained our property. In the early years we had had a problem with our Dun Laoghaire restaurant – we had had to terminate the franchise contract but could not easily get our sign back because the franchisee had paid for it himself when setting up. Experience is a hard school but we learned never to make the same mistakes twice.

Abrakebabra's franchisees made their profit from efficient management of their operations and attraction of customers into their restaurant in preference to rival operations. Franchisees were sold a guaranteed, tried-and-tested formula, offering a well-known and successful brand, quality products, bulk-buying benefits, group advertising and marketing and a network of head-office support services. No matter what difficulty or problem a new franchisee came up against we had usually come across it before and had dealt with it successfully. Each new franchisee was set up and their location fitted to the Abrakebabra restaurant specifications. In addition each franchisee was fully trained and given intensive support in the initial opening stages. All of these benefits contributed to enabling the franchisee to be more cost efficient than if they were a sole trader.

In return for these benefits the Abrakebabra franchisee must adhere to their side of the agreement. For all of the support that head office offers, the franchisee pays an initial set-up sum of usually £10,000, a continuous royalty fee and a contribution towards advertising costs. The royalty fee is 6 per cent of revenue (net of VAT) plus 1 per cent for advertising. In addition the franchisee must maintain the high standards laid out in Abrakebabra's operating guidelines. To protect the brand and group quality standards and to provide a continual quality service to the customer throughout all restaurants, each franchisee must run their operation in accordance with the company's guiding principles.

Each new franchisee was required to come up with £30,000 – about one-third of the total cost of a start-up. They took responsibility for running their restaurant on a day-to-day basis and any profits generated would go to them. We chose people who had commitment, who were prepared to put all their own money into the project and maybe even put their home up as collateral, because we knew that they were the most likely to succeed and to work hard. The typical successful franchisee turned out to be someone who was married, a settled house-holder who would put his or her heart and soul into the business. It was often a second career for them and some of the people had no experience at all of the fast-food business. In fact one of our best franchisees' previous employment had been in a bank. The worst of the early franchisees was an individual who had plenty of money and decided to set himself up as a fran-chisee. He didn't need to work and made a mess of the business by not being there.

We were having problems with managers. Even getting them to keep stock and cash sheets properly was difficult, whereas the franchisees found this task more enjoyable as they were dealing with their own assets. In the early days we set up the franchisees on a weekly standing order based on our estimate of what their turnover should be. We would take 7 per cent of that (net of VAT) and at the end of the month till reads would be checked and an adjustment made up or down. Sometimes we owed them money but generally they would send us a cheque for the bal-ance. So, in addition to the income generated by our own shops, we had money coming into our bank account from an increas-ing number of franchisees. The cash flow was good.

Increasingly, I saw the franchisees as being part of our family. In the widest sense they were our children. In their first year, I saw them as being like babies: they needed everything, we were a bit like their parents and they accepted all that we told them without question. After about five years, when they had learned to read and write, so to speak, they would start to do things on their own. Some years later, like progressing into their teens, they thought that they knew everything, much more than we did. After about ten years they were ready to leave home and wanted to do their own thing. We found that if we could keep them for ten years we were doing very well and that it took a very mature franchisee to realise the benefits of continuing the association with us beyond that period.

Abrakebabra's expansion through franchising meant that Graeme and I had to travel much more than we had when we just had our four restaurants in Dublin. We were constantly trying to locate new sites and endeavouring to select potential franchisees. In addition we had to ensure that each existing franchisee was visited on a regular basis.

When we had selected a city or town for a new restaurant we would usually place an advertisement in the local paper inviting interested parties to contact me at the Abrakebabra head office in Dublin to arrange a meeting. Sometimes we would approach an existing fast-food take-away operator and see if they would be interested in converting their business into an Abrakebabra. At this stage they would, of course, have known that an Abrakebabra would be in their area very soon and they had to consider carefully whether they wanted competition or were prepared to pay us 7 per cent of an increased turnover. Sometimes potential applicants would telephone us unprompted and enquire about becoming a franchisee, without having any particular location in mind.

Abrakebabra wrote the contract, the terms of which were non-negotiable because the company is the owner of the brand

and its associated trademarks. The essence of the contract was that the franchisee wants to use something that the franchisor owns and the franchisor has the benefit of knowledge and information that need not necessarily be disclosed to the franchisee. The agreement grants the franchisee exclusive rights to operate an Abrakebabra restaurant at an approved location and to use the company trademarks. The 6 per cent and 1 per cent fees are set out and franchisees are required to submit weekly turnover figures each Monday for their restaurant, now done by modem.

In addition to helping with site selection, franchisees have an assigned area supervisor who carries out regular visits. A quarterly newsletter is also produced by me at head office and is distributed to all franchisees, containing information on operational changes, current food prices, management advice and assistance. And if a franchisee has any issues they would like to be addressed they can contact their area supervisor or head office and assistance is available immediately.

In the meantime Helen and I had moved from Aranleigh to a house more in line with my newfound wealth: Stirling Park off Orwell Road, between Rathgar and Churchtown. Number 3 was a wonderful town house with red-brick facing and a spacious interior. I was even able to install a swimming-pool in the basement. It had everything that a young family required and it was conveniently situated to our head office in Rathmines. There was only one drawback: it was also near the embassy of the USSR, which had a round-the-clock security presence. This attracted the attention of a criminal gang that had begun to bait the Gardaí by carrying out criminal activities under their noses without being caught. The General had arrived on the scene. We, however, were blissfully unaware of this when we purchased our home; to us it was an idyllic setting in which to raise our family.

In a relatively short space of time we had moved from being a one- or two-restaurant operation to looking at sites for company shops or for franchisees, interviewing, assessing and searching-out potential franchisees and constantly checking up on existing restaurants. It was a demanding schedule for two brothers with a life outside of business. We needed help in managing what was becoming an empire. It was time to appoint a general manager.

CHAPTER 14

General managers and others

I N THE 1960S, after he had resigned as prime minister, the British statesman Harold Macmillan was asked what he had feared most during his years in politics. Was it, his interviewer probed, his opponents in his own Conservative Party or his ideological opponents in the Labour Party. The reply he gave, however, was quite different from what was expected of him: "Events, dear boy, events gave me the most trouble," Macmillan answered.

As the 1980s unfolded, Graeme and I discovered that managing a rapidly expanding business meant that we were on a very steep learning curve. Events, both inside and outside the business, shaped our lives and in many ways changed them. As I look back over twenty years, I recall a kaleidoscope of memories, some unpleasant and some downright nasty.

As the number of restaurants increased we felt the need to appoint someone who would have day-to-day responsibility for seeing that they were operating efficiently. We settled on an employee in one of the restaurants and gave him a van and instructions to keep in close contact with the restaurants to ensure that everything was OK. There might be, for instance, little or no stock when the 8 p.m. shift turned up for work or perhaps not all of the shift would have arrived. Stock had to be replenished, maybe from another restaurant, and people had to be found to fill the gaps. This, of course, was the restaurant manager's task but they could not be on the spot sixteen hours a day and they had to take holidays. A problem in moving stock from one location to another, to cater for an immediate need, is that the paperwork is not always completed and that led to further problems. He was basically a runner who did the job with little or no training but I suppose he was our first general manager.

For the first eight or nine years I was solely responsible for banking all the cash from our restaurants. We had at least one safe in each branch that needed to be opened once a week. At one stage I was collecting cash from nine shops, until I discovered that Securicor would do it for about £20 so they got the contract. However, in the meantime I did have some scary moments.

One day, on Aston Quay, I had two bags of money, containing about £10,000 – the contents of two safes. The turnover of our O'Connell Bridge restaurant was so great that we needed two safes there. I always made a point of carrying the money in Abrakebabra bags so that anyone who saw me would think that I was just carrying out food. The weight of the cash was so great that I had to double up the bags to be sure that they wouldn't tear. The plan was to bring them home and count the cash on our dining-room table. Our two older children helped me count it and thought it was all great fun – it probably also helped with the development of their mathematical skills.

As I returned to my car, a man approached me and tipped me on the shoulder. I immediately knew that I was about to be robbed and, thinking only of the company's assets and not at all about my own safety, I threw everything into the boot of my car and slammed it shut. Unfortunately for me, "everything" included my only set of car keys and the gentleman in question was just looking for directions to the GPO. Both of us were pretty scared for different reasons. Luckily I was in the AA and they came promptly and rescued me from my predicament.

Our Upper O'Connell Street restaurant was originally a franchise run by the Boyle brothers who, for reasons best known to themselves, had installed a cavern in their basement, complete with a safe door, into which they could lock themselves if there was any trouble. The brothers did not have the success that they anticipated and they sold the restaurant back to us. Early one morning Eamon Maguire, who was our manager in Donnybrook, was driving home through O'Connell Street when he spotted a van parked outside and two men inside the restaurant. As it was around 5 a.m. and the restaurant was closed, his suspicions were immediately aroused. On closer inspection it transpired that the men had drilled through the round double steelhead of the floor-safe set in concrete, inserted bars and, using a crow-bar and a lorry jack, had taken the head off. They were just removing the money when they saw that they were being observed. Within seconds they were gone and a robbery was foiled.

In another restaurant the safe was mysteriously filling with water, which had the effect of forcing the money to the top where it could be easily removed. Although we did not suspect him initially, the manager was doing this. He had not put the money into the safe in the first place and this was just a ruse to make us believe that there had been a robbery. We only discovered what was really happening when the manager's ex-wife squealed on him because he had not paid her alimony. After this we changed the rules so that two people, including the manager, had to co-sign the docket before the cash was dropped into the safe.

Our next general manager lasted for a couple of years until, by mutual consent, he moved on to pastures new and in the mid-1980s we acquired one of the best general managers that we ever had. Nicky Toppin had been a social worker with itinerant children, working with Victor Bewley's settlement committee. As the job required him to work late into the night, he often called into Wildes nightclub to relax after work. He became a regular and within months its owners asked him to manage the place. Nicky claims that he wasn't pushing to get the job but was, in fact, the only sober person in the club!

While managing Wildes, Nicky was approached by Graeme, through a mutual friend, with a view to him moving over to Abrakebabra. Graeme was impressed by what Nicky had done with Wildes but Nicky, a marketing graduate, did not intend to sell himself short. After a lot of negotiation we agreed that Nicky would come to Abrakebabra as general manager on a salary.

One of the initiatives he introduced to Abrakebabra was a computer programme he developed himself that analysed stock movement in relation to sales. With the programme, we were able to identify critical areas of waste and when we linked this information into the staff bonus system the gross profit immediately increased. He also crystallised the sales and wastage information from a twelve-page report to a two-page summary.

A general manager's job is nearly impossible, in that they are squeezed from both sides, i.e. from the side of the directors and of the staff. They have to hire and fire and in the meantime ensure that the restaurants are kept running smoothly. They have to iron out the everyday problems that are encountered and are always answerable to the directors. Nicky was very good at managing both Graeme and me and getting the best response from our staff.

Problems at the time included a small minority of staff who

were watering the sauces, buying their own pitta bread, only filling it with half the specified meat portion, selling it over the counter and taking the money home themselves. Apart from the loss of revenue, quality was suffering and our good name was being tarnished. We discovered this scam through the use of customer comment cards and mystery shoppers. These were people who went from restaurant to restaurant sampling the product and reporting back to the general manager. At the beginning we gave these mystery shoppers vouchers but it became evident to the staff at the different branches that they were not ordinary customers. When we gave them cash instead, the information we received was invaluable.

Customer comment cards were a great source of information on what was actually happening in each outlet. They also encouraged staff to wear their name-tags, as prizes were available to the staff members with the most plaudits from the customers. We designed the cards with little faces on them: happy, neither happy nor sad and sad. The customer simply ticked the appropriate face under headings such as speed of service, food quality and restaurant cleanliness. There was also a comment section, where customers could elaborate on certain issues if they wanted to. Obviously, one of the problems with this system was that certain managers could be tempted to discard cards with unfavourable comments. To counter this possibility we introduced a locked comment box and each week someone from head office would collect the cards and pass them on to the general manager.

One of the biggest problems encountered over the years was keeping track of our franchisees' turnover. Under the franchise agreement, as I have outlined, we were supposed to receive 6 per cent net of VAT (plus 1 per cent for advertising and marketing). Franchisees would ring in their turnover figures and we would carry out spot checks on individual restaurants. We guessed that a few of them may have been operating a second till.

Another way of checking was to look at their soft-drinks figures, which kept track of customer throughput. The gross profit that each restaurant should make was in the region of 64–67 per cent and if they were showing only 54 per cent you could be pretty certain that there was a error of some kind amounting to around 10 per cent.

As we were a cash-rich business we inevitably attracted the attentions of the criminal fraternity. For the first few years the restaurant managers would carry the wages back to their branches each week from head office. One of our managers, Robbie Kelly, was stopped at traffic-lights when two guys on a motorbike drew alongside, pointed a gun at him and demanded the cash. Needless to say he handed it over, they sped off and Robbie escaped with his life. We decided afterwards that the staff wages would be paid out of the safe in each restaurant and that no more cash would be carried around. Although this was a relatively minor incident it did remind us that we could be a target for criminals.

With tens of thousands of people using our restaurants every week, public-liability insurance was a big factor in our expenditure. It had rapidly increased from £10,000 to £60,000 in a very short time. We used brokers, of course, and one year we obtained a great deal from a Spanish company. However, when we made a claim we discovered that they were not registered to trade in Ireland. Always take the time to read the small print: it pays in the long run.

CHAPTER 15

More events

NICKY TOPPIN stayed with us, as general manager, for nearly six years and it was a mutually beneficial experience. When he moved on, he didn't move too far. In fact, he became a franchisee and opened his own Abrakebabra restaurant in 11 Lower Baggot Street. Number 11 turned out to be one of our most successful restaurants, catering as it did for the lunchtime, early evening and late-night trade, even though it was only 620 square feet. He subsequently acquired two further franchises in The Square, Tallaght, and South Anne Street, Dublin, and after a couple of years he also opened two Eddie Rocket's. Not content with this, in 1998 he took a lease on the former Irish Film Company premises on Lower Leeson Street and opened the Sugar Club, which has become a very successful music venue. His latest venture is into juice bars. I have remained good friends with Nicky. He is a restless entrepreneur who, having learned at the feet of the masters, is determined to leave his own mark on the franchise business.

Nicky Toppin was succeeded as general manager by Terry Jermyn and then by David Zebedee, who is still with Abrakebabra as an executive director.

One day while looking through the business pages of the national dailies we saw an advertisement offering fast-food restaurants for sale outside of Dublin. As we were always on the lookout for new business opportunities we asked our accountant to make an anonymous inquiry. It transpired that one of our franchisees was trying to sell on his restaurants, as he was entitled to do with our consent. The problem was there was a discrepancy in the figures that he was returning to us. The unsuspecting vendor went on to tell our accountant that the figures he was giving us were much lower. Not only had we taped the conversation but also we got his three-year figures from the company's office, which confirmed everything he had said. Confronted with this evidence he sold his franchise back to us for the amount that he should have given us based on his true turnover. Accurate figures from franchisees are an essential part of the business.

As I have said, our O'Connell Bridge restaurant had the highest turnover of all the company shops. It was so successful that we decided to open it 24 hours a day and introduced an excellent breakfast menu. Turnover went up but profit margins fell and it did not make sense until we realised that some of our staff from other restaurants were dropping into O'Connell Bridge for a cheap breakfast before heading off to work. There were also problems with equipment breaking down from being used continuously. Reluctantly, we reverted to the regular noon–4.30 a.m opening hours.

Soon after we opened O'Connell Bridge a window was broken. Shortly after that three young local lads turned up and inquired if the manager needed a security presence. I spoke with them and told them that if they were prepared to wear a uniform and carry out the usual security duties we would pay them a wage. Although I strongly suspected that they had something entirely different in mind, after some hesitation they agreed to my proposal and ended up working for us. They eventually set up their own security company and became quite successful.

In O'Connell Bridge also we had a break-in on the only day of the year that we were closed: Christmas Day. The intruders failed to open the safes but we then had to hire security personnel for this restaurant every Christmas.

Another security incident in Temple Bar was to cost us a lot of money. A security guard prevented a customer from entering because he thought that he was a well-known troublemaker. Unfortunately for us, he said this to the individual concerned and also to his companion. In fact it was a case of mistaken identity. The man happened to be a well-respected accountant and he sued us for slander. That cost us £30,000. The security guard thought that he was doing his job but he was a bit over-zealous.

In our Dun Laoghaire restaurant, late one evening, one of the customers pulled a seat apart with his bare hands, for no apparent reason. The response of the security men on duty was appalling. But they did not realise their actions were recorded on the CCTV equipment and again we had to settle by paying £30,000.

We had a better outcome in Baggot Street when a customer claimed that he had been beaten up on the premises and as a result his back was injured and he was unable to walk. We had had no security presence that night and were looking at a £60,000 claim. As a precaution, we employed a detective to follow this individual around and the detective produced photographs showing the man carrying his shopping up a hill. We also obtained evidence that he had driven from Kerry to Dublin to attend a GAA match. When we confronted him with these facts the case was dropped.

We discovered that in Dun Laoghaire one of the staff was giving free meals to taxi men in return for being driven back and forth to work, free of charge. I was out late one night and went along to the Abrakebabra on George's Street in the middle of Dun Laoghaire for a meal. I was waiting in the queue and the guy in front of me, when asked to pay, said, "I'm a taxi man. I get mine free."

When it came to my turn to pay, I asked the staff member, "Why don't I get a free meal?"

"Well," she said, "you're not a taxi man."

"You are quite right," I replied. "I'm the owner."

She nearly dropped dead. The staff member was reprimanded and the manager was fired. This proved that it was only by going around the restaurants yourself and seeing what it was like on the ground that you could get an accurate idea of what was happening. Obviously Abrakebabra now has many resources at its disposal and these kinds of incidents do not happen but in the early years we were running everything ourselves and had limited resources of time, people and money.

At home, Helen was looking after our family while continuing her involvement with the WPA. David and Ros were attending The High School, Danum which was near to our home in Rathgar. Rosalind later went to St Andrews College to sit her Leaving Certificate, a reverse of what happened to me. Family life continued as normal until one morning a neighbour called to inform me that all the tyres of the cars on our park had been slashed during the night. I emerged to discover that all eight tyres of our cars had been destroyed. This had happened in the park on a previous occasion but it was our introduction to organised crime in Dublin. While nothing could be proved, the view was that the Dublin criminal Martin Cahill, known as the General, was the mastermind behind the operation. The residents of Stirling Park were not the targets, however. The real target was the Gardaí, who were nearby and totally unaware of what was happening. The object was to hold them up to ridicule and we certainly did not think we were getting the protection we felt entitled to. We were not the only residential area to suffer this attack but when it happens to you the feeling of helplessness and vulnerability really hits home. But worse was to come.

Back on the company front, by 1989 we had twenty restaurants throughout Ireland, about half of which were company owned, while at the time McDonald's, our main competitor, had only ten. Abrakebabra competed with its rivals on two levels. On one hand we competed for customers by endeavouring to offer the best quality food at the most competitive prices while on the other hand we competed continuously to attract and retain the best franchisees.

We also had to compete with smaller sole traders, such as the traditional chippers. One way of dealing with this kind of competition was to convert them into Abrakebabra franchisees. Graeme and I needed to be out and about, checking on our own shops and on our franchisees and seeking out new outlets. We needed to be mobile. Given the condition of Irish roads in the early 1990s it was difficult to mention mobility and car in the same breath. So we decided to take to the air by buying a share in a helicopter.

We bought a share in an Enstrom, a small blue and white three-seater craft, for a total coat of about £80,000. Graeme was very enthusiastic about learning to pilot it and I was sucked into the slipstream of excitement that surrounded the purchase. We both took lessons and the idea was that, as we had or wanted to have Abrakebabra restaurants in nearly every town in Ireland with a population of over 10,000, a helicopter would give us the right image of successful go-ahead businessmen. In turn, we hoped this would help to attract the very best franchisees. Even today, arriving in a helicopter brings with it a certain cachet. But in the early

1990s, before the Celtic Tiger had begun to roam the land, a helicopter really set you apart. It would, we expected, be the most efficient way to travel the length and breadth of the country.

Our flying instructor, Colin Sayers, was a bit like a Second World War pilot. He was from the old school of instructors: you did exactly what you were told and didn't ask questions. One day I was learning to hover ten feet off the ground and facing into a strong gale. Every time the helicopter would start to go backwards I had to kick on one of the pedals and press the joystick forward. Colin was sitting beside me in the cockpit with a buddy stick but I was in control. Colin told me to keep the craft level but, after over five minutes of pressing and kicking, I began to tire and to forget which pedal to kick. If you make a mistake at ten feet off the ground and the blades strike land you are in deep trouble.

I turned to Colin and said, "Please take over – I can't control it."

"You can: think, think," he replied.

The wind velocity was increasing and I knew that if I kept the controls for another minute we would crash.

I said again, "Please take over," and again he declined.

The third time I said, "I'm taking my hands and feet off the controls. Please take over."

I lifted both feet in the air and raised my hands above my head. Colin turned utterly white and quickly took over and landed. He had not realised that I had completely lost control of the craft. We looked at each other for a long time before either of us spoke and I never tried to fly a helicopter again.

Even with a pilot there were problems. It turned out that nearly every time we wanted to use the helicopter there was either fog, gale warnings or it was being repaired – all of which meant that we could not use it. The procedure in flying craft is that you routinely replace parts long before they wear out. Over the time we had the helicopter we must have replaced nearly the entire machine.

I remember one instance when we were flying to Derry to see the newly opened RAP packaging facility and got caught in a 60 m.p.h. gale. Graeme was asleep beside me and I looked down to the ground and could see that the lorries below were going faster than we were. In reality our airspeed was probably about 20 m.p.h. That day our engine blew a gasket and we suffered an oil leak. We had an excellent pilot, however, in Ms Darra Fitzgerald, who now pilots the Sikorski rescue helicopter in the west of Ireland. We were over Lough Erne and Darra asked me to try to identify an RAF landing strip so that we could get down quickly. I managed to find it and she took us down safely.

Shortly after my last piloting experience the helicopter crashed with Christy O'Connor Junior in it. He escaped uninjured and won a European tour event the following weekend. Darra was piloting it at the time and thanks to her skill in handling the crash landing no one was seriously injured. Counting ourselves very lucky, we took the insurance money and did not replace the Enstrom.

Back on earth we had opened the River Club, a nightclub and restaurant above our Abrakebabra at Merchants' Arch, beside the Ha'penny Bridge in Temple Bar, Dublin. At first it was a success, attracting an up-market clientele, such as Mel Gibson when he was filming Braveheart. Mel was a very interesting and charming man and an excellent conversationalist. Brad Pitt once asked me to keep the women away from him and Bono and his wife Ali used to come and sit behind our grand piano. Pierce Brosnan turned up after a Bond premiere and told me, as I sat at his table, that he loved kebabs and liked to eat them in his home town of Navan.

Findlaters told us that we had the largest order of champagne per week for any club or pub in Dublin. To emphasise this record we built a gallery on the second floor and called it the Champagne Bar, where only the bubbly stuff could be consumed. Unfortunately the River Club was too exclusive and in the long term didn't really catch on. We sold it on at a small profit and now it is a thriving nightclub catering for twenty-somethings.

The River Club was at the top of Merchants' Arch, where the merchants of Dublin held their meetings. In fitting out the building we were careful to keep the original windows and granite facings. One day our cleaning lady informed us that she had seen a ghost. Around the same time a very heavy statue fell from one of the alcoves and was smashed. Nobody was injured and after a while I forgot both incidents.

Two years later, one of our staff members ran out of the basement shouting that he had seen a ghost-like figure. I asked him to draw it and he drew a picture of a headless monk with a rope around his waist. The apparition also lacked feet. It appeared to be leaning behind the counter beside the Pepsi machine. We wondered if the staff member was suffering from lack of sleep or had taken something stronger than Pepsi. But you never really know. Strangely, the picture that he drew corresponded closely to the description that the cleaning lady had given me two years previously. In order not to alarm anyone, I had asked her not to repeat her story and had kept quiet myself about the whole event.

Merchants' Arch is a very old building and, as I say, you can never be quite sure.

CHAPTER 16

The armed robbery

ONE OF THE benefits of running a business like Abrakebabra was that I did not have to be at my desk until after 10 a.m. The other side of the coin, however, was that, as the restaurants stayed open until 4 a.m., it was necessary to have a management presence on hand late at night to deal with problems as they arose. While Graeme and I and our general manager shared the late-night duties, it was sometimes difficult to get away in the evenings. Colleagues needed to be talked to in a social setting and increasingly I was unable to be at home with my family as much as I would have wished.

The events of September 1989 are etched in my memory, not because I was there, but because I was not there. I played a walk-on part in a drama that has deeply affected all the members of my family. My daughter, Ros, was there in 3 Stirling Park on that dreadful night and it is through her words that this part of the story must be told. I am very grateful to Ros for revisiting that frightening episode in her mind and for giving her account of the traumatic events that engulfed us that night.

It was Tuesday 26 September 1989 and from about 9 p.m. onwards Emma, our little Cavalier King Charles, had been restless and barking frantically in the back garden. Mum, my two brothers, David and Jeff, and myself were all at home. Jeff had reluctantly been put to bed; David was in his room reading. Dad was out doing his rounds of the Abrakebabra restaurants, carrying out his routine nightly checks.

Emma, by about 10.30 p.m., was refusing to come in from the garden and was barking so madly that Mum was giving out to her and had to shoo her in with a garden brush. The dog had only ever got this disturbed over a certain fat, marmalade cat who used to sit on the wall and taunt the physically fragile and highly strung dog.

I had school the next morning; having just starting in 1st year in The High School it was bedtime by 11 p.m. I remember making my way up to bed, my room being at the front of the house. The dog was still barking but Mum had closed the door into the kitchen. However, Emma was still barking from the hall, stairs and landing. I was getting very annoyed with her, as she wasn't letting up. Finally to try and calm her down I took her back into the kitchen. She barked for a while longer and then finally ... silence.

I thought nothing of all the commotion and again put it down to that stupid fat cat. The last real task that I remember, before the night's surreal events began to unfold, was setting my alarm clock. It was 11.13 p.m. when I sat on my bed. This precise time has stayed with me since that night. It was locked onto my alarm clock until the next day when I re-entered my bedroom and since that night I have never gone to bed before 11.13 p.m. Neither have I slept with my bedroom door unlocked, ever ...

I was sitting on my bed setting the alarm and my door was opened. All I saw was a dark figure, a man with a balaclava and a gun pointed directly at me. He stood in the crack of the door with the lights from the landing spilling about his silhouette. He was waving the gun to signal me to come to him. I sat there and all I thought was that Dad must have come home early and he must be playing a trick on Mum or David. He kept waving the gun for me to move and then he froze. I also froze in that second, realising that something was about to happen. The next moment another man also with a gun and a balaclava brought David into my bedroom covered by a bed sheet. At that moment I knew that this was very real and felt the slow heart-stopping realisation of abject fear. We were both placed under the sheet and I could hear one of the men closing the curtains and saw for myself our house landing lights being turned off from beneath the sheet. I remember feeling totally alone, as the closing of the curtains shut out all hope of help and all thoughts of the outside world.

David and myself were walked down to Mum and Dad's bedroom where Mum was standing, and we were all brought straight into the *en suite* bathroom. We realised that they had left my younger brother Jeff asleep and I didn't want to think what they had done to little Emma.

Mum kept asking about Jeff and begged them to leave him asleep. Funny, as he was a baby and it was about 5 years later that we actually told Jeff that there had been an armed robbery. For a few hours he had refused to believe us. I mean who would ...?

So there we sat, the three of us on the edge of the bath. A third armed robber, slightly older and fatter, sat with us for the duration of the hold-up, also on the bath near the doorway.

I found out later on that the second masked robber had entered David's room and just like me David had thought it was Dad playing a practical joke. David had been reading in bed, with a sidelight on and the armed robber came right into David's bedroom and silently put a gun to his head, saying "Come to your Mother's room". The masked man grabbed a sheet, put it over David and instead brought him into my room.

At the same time as the other two robbers were approaching David and myself, Mum was in bed. The third armed robber appeared at her bedroom door. She thought it was David in the doorway, as she was half asleep and couldn't properly see the outline of the figure.

She said, "David, I'm nearly asleep, what is it?"

The armed robber said, "This is not David, this is for real, take it easy, get out of bed, are you covered?"

Mum said that thoughts raced through her head. She had a couple of seconds to press the panic alarm button beside her bed but as she thought about it, at that moment both David and I were led with a sheet covering us into the bedroom and that is what stopped her.

The three of us were ushered silently into the *en suite* bathroom and the sheet was removed from our heads. The third, older armed robber stayed with us, as the other two men ransacked the rest of the house. We all sat there in silence on the edge of the bath, not moving and trying to calm ourselves. I sat there shaking, praying as the stark reality of what was actually happening began to sink in. I was convinced that we would be hurt or taken away. The threat of death was very much on my mind. There had been a spate of kidnappings by the General's men and the thought was never far from my mind.

I asked about Emma and was told she was fine. To a thirteen-year-old girl the well-being of her beloved pet is just as important as the safety of her family. My Mum talked to the masked man holding us hostage in the cramped bathroom. He seemed to be a lot more relaxed and in control than the other two men, who kept coming in and out of the bathroom frantically asking him questions and whispering information into his ear. He was friendly and pleasant despite the circumstances, and even referred to being tired and the annoyance of having to get up for work the next morning!?! Friendly, except that he still held his gun, an item there to remind us, no matter how loosely held, that he was our captor and we were at his mercy.

During this time our thoughts turned to Dad: what would happen if he arrived home, did they already have him, having captured him earlier? Was this whole event to kidnap him? One of the most frightening and tension filled moments was when one of the other two masked men came into the bathroom. One of them was highly charged and in a mad and panicked way said they had found a shot gun, where were the cartridges and where the hell were the keys to the safe (located in the basement beside the swimming pool). The next second, they brought my brother David out of the room alone. I was frantic with fear, what were they doing, what were they going to do with him, was he going to come back? They held him outside for what seemed like an eternity and finally brought him back. I breathed thank god, but then to my horror they took my Mother away. I started to panic, shake and felt like I was going to choke. Please don't hurt her ... I calmed myself thinking that if they brought David back in the she would be fine. Suddenly it occurred to me that I was next. What were they doing, please god don't let them take me ...

Mum was brought back in and they decided that they didn't need to take me out. I found out later that they had questioned both my Mum and David about the whereabouts of the shot-gun's cartridges and the location of the Basement's Safe keys. Neither my Mum nor brother knew the answer and thankfully the robbers believed them. I mean, Dad was the only person who knew where both items were. Mum and David individually told the raiders that the safe was empty and there was nothing in it. It was the truth and to this day no reason explains why they believed them.

We remained held in the bathroom for what seemed like an eternity, there seemed no end to this ordeal ... how would they leave us? After momentary exchanges of conversation with our captor and more interruptions from the other two masked men, finally they asked about my Father, where was he, when was he expected home. Mum told them that he was out checking on the shops and said that he usually was home by 1 a.m. In my mind time was irrelevant and I had no idea whether we had been there for an hour or the whole night. I began to shiver again both from fear and the cold. I was only wearing a summer nightdress and the huddling of Mum, David and myself wasn't enough to keep me warm.

The third masked man came in to the bathroom again and asked if we needed some water or some warm blankets. The other member of the group appeared with a rack of some of Dad's ties and proceeded to tie all our legs up and tie our arms behind our backs. Then all three robbers left us alone and ungagged and said that they would be back up with some water. The bathroom door was locked. The key taken from the door. For the first time we were left alone, just the three of us without one of the robbers. However, instead of moving or trying to escape all three of us believed that they were still in the house and that any second one of them would be back to watch over us again. We just whispered to each other, I can't remember what exactly, just some reassurances and coupled with the comforting phrase of a Mother, "Don't be afraid, it's going to be ok". Again for what seemed like hours, we sat in virtual silence until we heard someone calling us … it was Dad.

I remember Mum started to shout, "Wyn we are in the bathroom". After a few moments scuffling, the bathroom door was unlocked and a bewildered Dad stood there. By this time I had managed to untie myself and kept asking for Emma, Mum was asking for Jeff. I ran downstairs to find the dog knocked out but alive. Mum ran into Jeff and woke him up, he was perfectly fine and untouched both physically and mentally from the dramatic events.

That night I remember that the house was swarming with police. I gave a statement to the police. The next day, again more police came and took fingerprints. Mum and Dad decided not to release the event to the press. The two prominent theories about who carried out the raid were either that of the IRA or the General's men (we were living in Rathgar and at that time the General lived in close proximity in Rathmines). Of the valuables stolen, Mum's jewellery and precious irreplaceable family heirlooms and silver were taken. However, perhaps one of the most precious and irreplaceable items stolen was that of our feelings of security, safety and innocence. The armed robbery left on all of us a scar and a fear that will never be forgotten. An event that lasted a number of hours will remain and affect us for the rest of our lives.

As Ros has written, when I had finished doing the rounds of the restaurants I returned home around 1 a.m. I was immediately struck by how unnaturally quiet and still our home was. No light was visible and the normally barking Emma was silent. I looked in on Jeff, as I usually did before retiring, and he was sleeping peacefully. When I looked into Ros' and David's rooms neither were there and the beds looked as if they had been disturbed. Our room was completely empty. I called out Helen's name a couple of times.

Then I heard muffled shouts from the direction of our *en suite* bathroom. It took me a couple of minutes to find the key and when I opened the door I was horrified to find Helen, David and Ros tied hand and foot sitting on the edge of our bath.

I immediately called the Gardaí and they were at the house within minutes. I was pleased that no one had been physically injured but dismayed to discover that all of the Beere family heirlooms had been taken. None of these were ever recovered.

On the balance of probabilities and the presence of the older and fatter man the Gardaí told me that they thought the raid was the work of the General.

Nearly five years later Martin Cahill, also known as the General, was gunned down on the corner of Oxford Road and Charleston Road in Ranelagh as he waited at a stop sign in his car. He was on his way to return a video that he had rented the day before. It is believed that the Provisional IRA murdered him.

All of us suffered in different ways from the traumatic events of that September night in 1989. My wife Helen blamed me for having the ostentatious wealth that attracted the General and I believe this was a contributing cause to the breakdown of our marriage soon after. David was the eldest male in the house at the time, although he was only seventeen, and he perhaps felt that he could have done something more to protect his mother and sister. He could not, of course, without endangering his own and their safety but the helplessness of the situation he found himself in has been a burden to him since. Ros, as she has told us, sleeps with her bedroom door locked and never retires before 11.13 p.m. And I have had to live with the guilt of not having been there to protect my family. I suspect there was very little I could have done against such determined armed robbers but I would have liked to have been in a position to try.

Victims everywhere have been traumatised as we have been. Counselling can help but it is an unfortunate fact that, like it or not, you are never the same person after the event as you were before it.

CHAPTER 17

Spending the
1 per cent

THE 1 PER CENT of franchisees' turnover paid to us for advertising and marketing has always been a bone of contention. In the early years when there were fewer restaurants it was not a very significant sum but as the empire developed it became a budget to be reckoned with. Sometimes the franchisees thought we were keeping it for ourselves. At all times it was strictly ring fenced and kept separate from the 6 per cent (net of VAT) payable to us as franchisers but it still caused problems.

Advertising is generally expected to fulfil several very different tasks, sometimes simultaneously. These include the desire to promote a new brand, to entice additional people to sample an established brand, to encourage that brand's existing clientele to remain faithful, to tempt existing customers to purchase more product and to encourage buyers to pay more.

In the early days, we found that radio advertising was the most effective method of getting our message across and reaching a larger audience for the limited budget that was at our disposal. About 80 per cent of our customers were aged between 15 and 35. TV advertising was very expensive – about £2,000 for a

1. Samantha Mumba with
   Shirley and myself at a
   UNICEF lunch. *(left)*

2. Gerry Ryan of RTÉ with
   Yvonne Ellard, Miss Ireland,
   alongside my Ferrari at the
   time of the Abrakebabra
   Holiday promotion. *(below)*

3. Shirley, Colm Meaney and myself at Dublin Castle. *(above)*

4. Me and Angel at the All White Charity event. *(right)*

5. My vintage MGA 1956 in racing green.

6. With An Taoiseach Bertie Ahern, TD, and Shirley at a charity ball in the Radisson Hotel.

7. With Claudia Carroll, of *Fair City*, and Angel.

8. Pat Kenny of RTÉ with Caroline Morahan, now with *Off the Rails*, at the launch of our new bio-degradable packaging.

9. My 1991 Ferrari 348TS in London.

10. With the Liam McCarthy Cup following Offaly's triumph in the All Ireland Hurling Final. *From left* me, Offaly Captain Hubert Rigney and Manager Michael Bond.

11. Paul Kerr, Shirley and myself at Palmerston De La Salle October 2004.

12. The Enstrom helicopter before it crashed.

13. My Aquador speed boat for fishing and fun.

14. Myself, Charlie McCreevy, TD, and Angel as Marilyn Monroe at the opening of the 50th Abrakebabra Restaurant in Kildare Town. (*above*)

15. My Harley Davidson and Ferrari at home. (*above*)

16. Mr Justice Fergus M. Flood, retired, with his beloved dog. (*right*)

17. Ann Boylan, Miss World Rosanna Davidson and Shirley, 2003. (*below*)

7

18. The three pyramids of Egypt, Shirley, me and Gavin's head.

19. In a dugout canoe on the Monkey River in Belize 2003.

20. The Pitons of St Lucia taken during a wonderful holiday Shirley and I had with our friends Martin and Anne Whelan Devaux. *(above)*

21. Island in Guatemala 2003. *(above left)*

22. A tree dripping with orchids and bromeliads in Belize. *(above right)*

23. The Black Orchid, *Encyclia Cochleata*, the national flower of Belize. *(left)*

24. The three foot Wild Marsh Orchid *Dachylohriza Fuchsii* in the Kilternan field that I intend to save. By kind permission of *The Irish Times*.

25. The *Vanda Rothschildiana* Orchid. This is the third year that it has flowered for me.

26. The Cockle Shell Orchid. *(far left)*

27. The Irish Butterfly Orchid *Platanthera Bifolia*. *(left)*

28. The Slipper Orchid *Paphiopedilum Jack Flash* purchased at the London Orchid Show. *(far left)*

29. The Slipper Orchid *Paphiopedilum Prime Child*. *(left)*

30. My orchid greenhouse heated all the year around.

31. The beautiful Red Admiral butterfly on *Buddleia Davidii*, the butterfly bush.

32. Painted Lady butterfly, in my garden in Kilternan.

33. Peacock butterfly on *Buddleia Davidii*. Note the eye spots on the wings to fool the birds.

34. Eddie Irvine testing my Toyota Supra at
    Mondello Racetrack, 1995. *(above)*

35. Myself and Keith Duffy
    of Boyzone and
    Coronation Street
    fame. *(above right)*

36. My eldest son David
    and I at his graduation,
    Maynooth College,
    County Kildare. *(right)*

37. Ian, Graeme and myself dressed as vicars at Graeme's 40th birthday in 1998.

38. My daughter Rosalind and myself at her graduation at Trinity College Dublin.

39. The boys, David, Jeff, baby Gavin and me at my log cabin in Glencree Valley. *(above)*

40. Shirley, me and Gavin at his First Communion, 2004. *(right)*

41. The Beere and Rosney clan at Gavin's First Communion 29 May 2004.

fifteen-second slot – and we were pretty certain that the people who frequented our restaurants listened mostly to the radio. Gerry Ryan plugged us a lot on 2FM because we gave out car stickers, free of charge, which could be put on your back window. If they were spotted by the 2FM team your registration number would be announced on the radio and the winner would have about an hour to ring up and claim their prize, which was usually cash. This was a hugely successful campaign and I think we were one of the first companies to use this type of advertising. I still see some cars with Abrakebabra stickers on their back window.

We would meet with the franchisees and canvass suggestions from them regarding the type of advertising that they thought would be best. However, we soon discovered that there were as many opinions as franchisees and it was not a viable way of choosing an advertising strategy. Instead, we asked different advertising agencies to pitch for our business and chose one. They would then come up with plans for a campaign and we would go to the franchisees and see what they thought of it. If some element of the proposed campaign was not being accepted by many of our franchisees then we would be open to their input and perhaps alter or change the concept completely.

We viewed ourselves as sleek and fast paced so what better to portray this image than a racing car, which would appeal particularly to the youth market. We built up a relationship with the racing driver Vivian Daly and put the Abrakebabra logo on Vivian's two-litre Opel Lotus Formula 3 racing car. Even though he had only one eye, he was a fantastic driver and together we won many championships. At the Phoenix Park motor races we organised a hospitality marquee and brought on board 2FM, Statoil and Pepsi as co-sponsors, but the car was still known as the Abrakebabra car. We raced at Mondello also and used the venue to bring our franchisees out for a day's fun – in this regard it was very success-ful. We also incorporated our racing car into our car-sticker logo.

A racing car was perfect to use our logo on because Abrakebabra is such a long name. Other forms of sport did not lend themselves so easily to being branded in this fashion. For instance, we sponsored the Irish surfing champion and were able to have our logo on his board but swimmers that contacted us couldn't really offer any space long enough to be used effectively. We did, however, sponsor a skydiver who had our logo embla-zoned on his paraglider. Soccer teams, both regional and local, also benefited.

In 1996 we sponsored the Irish cycling team in the round-Ireland Milk Rás. They finished second and we had great cover-age throughout the event. I happened to be visiting our Castlebar restaurant as the Rás passed and got an excellent photograph featuring the cyclists and the local Abrakebabra.

Being a champion swimmer myself, albeit at local level, I was delighted to be able to sponsor Michele Smith for her trip to swimming championships in Edinburgh. I had got to know her dad when I carried out a valuation of their family home in Rathcoole and I have seen the dedication that he, Michele and all her family have shown over the years in reaching the highest standards in her sport. I was very proud of her when she won three gold medals at the Atlanta Olympics.

We also used the staff uniform to reinforce brand awareness. The decision to have a uniform was a considered one. McDonald's had one and we followed their example. The uniform was bright and trendy and a baseball cap gave staff a youthful look. The managers wore shirts and the name-badges distinguished them. The staff never liked wearing name-badges because if a customer were unhappy they would be able to refer to the per-son that served them by name. I got around this reluctance by introducing an Employee of the Month award that required the customers to praise good service by naming staff on the comment card. With prizes such as video recorders, TVs and stereos on offer we soon got an amazing improvement in the use of name-badges.

When uniforms were first introduced they were considered so attractive that they began to walk out of the restaurants. To counteract this, staff were required to pay a deposit that was refundable when they were leaving our employment.

One of the pluses in owning a chain of restaurants is that, from time to time, you get the chance to give money away. In one year we gave away 40 holidays as prizes. We tried, as far as possible, to link the trips into the international aspect of our menu. Hamburgers come from the US, kebabs from Turkey, baguettes from France, so we sent the prizewinners to these countries.

By this time Pepsi were giving us an annual contribution towards our advertising budget, no doubt to ensure our continued loyalty to their brand. In one year their contribution was £250,000 and together with the 1 per cent from our franchisees it enabled us to move seriously onto TV.

We had already had a cartoon campaign on TV that was relatively inexpensive and featured a sneaky-snake-type character. Before that we had just featured photographs of our restaurants and the product range with a background jingle. The cartoon incorporated a wand that would swipe across the screen and, as if by magic, a different Abrakebabra product would appear. But, unfortunately, the viewers didn't realise what they were seeing was supposed to be a magic wand: they thought that they were looking at a windscreen wiper, because up to that point the racing car had been a main focus of brand awareness.

We learned quickly that a proper TV advertisement with

equity members taking part would be the most effective. At this time we moved to Young Advertising. They knew exactly what we wanted and were able to come up with a great advertising strategy. We used the song "He's got the whole world in his hands" and the idea was to convey the variety of global cuisine available from Abrakebabra. We achieved this by having a French-looking woman holding a baguette, an obviously Turkish person with a kebab and an American with a burger. I went out to Ardmore Studios when it was being made, which was great fun. I learned a bit about making a film and also gained a lot of respect for the professionalism and skill of the people involved in the production.

We ran the advertisement on RTÉ One, Network 2 and on Sky One and it cost about £200,000 to make the twenty-second video clip. However, we could see the results immediately. Turnovers went up all around the country and people would say, "You've gone international. I've seen your ad on the telly." People started to talk about us and the financial community, in particular, saw us as having arrived and as being a credible competitor to McDonald's, whereas beforehand our image was that we were a smaller company, owned by Arabs. It was a major breakthrough because, for years, we had been perceived as not being an Irish company. Even today some people still think that Arabs run Abrakebabra.

Thanks to this and other campaigns run by Young Advertising, Abrakebabra is now one of the most recognised brands in Ireland and is up there with McDonald's, Bewley's and Guinness. We found Young Advertisng to be exceptional in their handling of our account.

One night at RTÉ after a Late Late Show I was having a drink in the green room and I got talking to Gay Byrne's right-hand woman, Maura Connolly. I suggested that Abrakebabra put up a car for a prize in a postal quiz on the show. She declined, saying they were fully sponsored for the foreseeable future. I persevered, however, and over the next weeks and months kept in touch with her, reminding her of my idea. I eventually got an agreement that we would offer a Rover car as a prize and Stuart Motors came on board by selling it to us at half price because of the publicity it would generate on the Late Late. We had the Abrakebabra logo on the licence plate and it was prominently featured during the show.

The time came to draw a card from the enormous pile of entries that had been sent in. The poet Brendan Kennelly, who was a guest on the show, drew one and Gay rang the sender to ask the easy question they still had to answer to claim the car. A woman answered but her husband had sent in the card and he was out playing tennis at his club. Brendan drew again and the number in Cork was answered by a woman. Gay spoke to her and asked her, by means of introduction, had she been watching the show. After a silence, she said, no, she hadn't. She then added that her daughter had died the night before. For the only time in my life watching the *Late Late Show* Gay Byrne was completely lost for words. He eventually said that he had better not continue. He offered his condolences and was preparing to terminate the call when the woman said that her late daughter would have wanted her to participate. She went on to answer the question correctly and won the Rover. The woman's late daughter had posted the card for her.

Brendan Kennelly then read a poem that captured the moment perfectly. I had the car delivered to Cork and the woman gave it to one of her other children, who was of driving age. It was a very sad and moving occasion and one that everybody who saw it remembers.

Another way to keep our name in front of the public was to put posters on bus shelters. When we went nationwide we discovered that this was an excellent form of advertising, in that they could be used throughout the country. £70,000 gave us 90 sites for 2 months, which was very good value.

One of our objectives in running the TV campaign was to endeavour to change our image from a solely late-night venue to a restaurant that could be used all day. We had a lot of sites close to office locations, such as Upper and Lower Baggot Street, South Anne Street and O'Connell Street and Bridge. The campaign helped to build up our luncheon and early evening trade and by timing it to coincide with troughs in our business, such as January, we were able to increase turnover where things previously had been a bit slow.

An alternative way of introducing people to the delights of our cuisine was to give them complimentary cards. These were first used in the very early days of the business and, without control, they ended up being abused. Eventually my signature had to be on all the cards and we gave them out as a reward and to get people into our restaurants. For instance, to entice people into the newly opened Abrakebabra at Merchants' Arch in Dublin we had a girl dressed-up as a burger giving cards out to passers-by. Some might entitle the bearer to a free drink with a meal or a two-for-the-price-of-one meal. It was all about getting people to taste the product and suppliers would support new outlets by contributing to the cost of the promotion.

Another promotional scheme was to give out free kebabs when a new restaurant opened. The kebab suppliers assisted us with this promotion and there would be queues along the pavement and the local publicity was tremendous. Or we might give a donation of £1 to a local cause, usually a hospital, for each kebab sold during the first week of trading. It was a great way to raise money for good causes and to get people to sample our menu. It told people that Abrakebabra had arrived in a locality and that we and the local franchisee were going to support the local community.

We did find, though, that staff were under a great strain during that first promotional week and would be extremely tired at the end of it. The restaurant would also be seriously depleted in terms of resources and stock. The franchisee would essentially forego making any money in that first week and a negative consequence would be that many of the staff would call in sick the following week when they were really needed and the restaurant was operating for profit.

One year we raised £10,000 for Live Aid and other monies for the ISPCC and the Variety Club of Ireland. Every week we would receive requests for donations to charity and, unfortunately, you have to say no to most and select just a few for support. In later years we ended up channelling all requests through our advertising agency, who would compile a list from which we would choose which charities to support. This left us free to get on with the business of running our company.

CHAPTER 18

Nearly went under

THE EARLY 1990S were not a great time for me, business wise and personally. The economy was faltering and people had less disposable income. Consequently, they tended to socialise less and less during the week, preferring to keep their scarce funds for the weekend. The market was also more competitive than it had been when we started in 1982. Other business people had seen how successful we were and, quite naturally, they wanted their slice of the action too.

One of these was Niall Fortune, who created the franchise for Eddie Rocket's in Ireland. He started in South Anne Street in Dublin and later franchised out sixteen restaurants, rather like us. Niall was quite up-front in his analysis of how to generate growth in his business: set up beside an Abrakebabra restaurant. He carried out this strategy on a number of sites and was doing very well while our turnovers were not increasing.

In 1994 we decided to open a fast-food restaurant on the ground floor of the Merchants' Arch building below the River Club in Temple Bar. We thought that it would be a good idea to see if an Eddie Rocket's restaurant would be a better bet than one of our own. The fit-out was much more expensive and on top of that we had to pay a franchise fee to Niall. The product at Eddie Rocket's is more expensive than in Abrakebabra and unfortunately for us it was not a good choice – from day one we consistently lost money on it. After about a year we gave up and converted it into an Abrakebabra and immediately it was a great success. For some reason, that was not a good site for an Eddie Rocket's. We did, however, learn how they went about their business and it was somewhat different from our model: their menu and seating were different and chrome fittings were very much to the fore.

Back in 1991, our turnovers had been falling for about six months. We looked carefully at what we had been doing and decided that if we were losing money and our competitor next door was making a profit then maybe we needed to revamp our image and our menu to take account of changing tastes. Our plan was to make the changes in the Donnybrook restaurant and monitor their effect on turnover and profit levels. If they turned out to be successful then we intended to roll them out through the whole network. But to carry out the revamp we needed money.

At the time we had an overdraft facility with the Bank of Ireland for £50,000 and we wanted to increase it to £70,000. Our good friend Christy Hayes had moved on but we were confident that our plans would be accepted and the increase would be forthcoming. The new manager looked at the figures that we had supplied and listened carefully to our accurate and truthful description of where we were in business terms. He then told us that not only would he not give us an increase in the overdraft facility but also, as we had no collateral, he intended to call it in forthwith. He went on to offer the gratuitous information that in his opinion we would be bust in three months.

We were taken aback by this approach. We had been good customers of the branch for nine years, had put millions through it and had never defaulted on any responsibilities that we had.

We learned a hard lesson that day. Our objective had been to set out clearly where we were and where we wanted to be and how we intended to get there. This was obviously a mistake and we subsequently learned that a little less emphasis on where we were and more emphasis on the Promised Land that we were heading for might have been a better idea. However, we would not have any overdraft facility if we did not obtain some collateral quickly. Our mother agreed to put up her home to guarantee the overdraft and at least we were still in business.

But we still had not obtained the finance needed to revamp the Donnybrook restaurant to see if that was the way forward that would restore our fortunes. Luckily enough Graeme played polo with Craig McKinney of Woodchester Finance and from the time we had started in business we had leased all our equipment from them. We went to Woodchester and they readily agreed to finance the new fit-out in Donnybrook. When it had been completed we also changed our whole menu.

Up to that point, apart from kebabs, burgers and chips there was little else to be had in an Abrakebabra. Now we introduced a whole new menu including baguettes. Imported from France as frozen dough, they were placed in a small oven and baked for four minutes. What came out was delicious and a great hit with the customers. The eleven-inch chicken baguettes with salads, sweet peppers and sauces began to rival our traditional kebabs and, along with other additions to our menu, put us once more on the road to success.

Our turnover and profits rose immediately in Donnybrook and we then knew what we had to do to survive and prosper. Over the next couple of years we revamped all our restaurants in turn and invariably the new look and the more extensive menu drew in the customers in ever-greater numbers.

Another bank that made our lives difficult at that time was

ABN. When we had bought out the freeholds on our own restaurants, as they became available, we borrowed money from ABN. By 1991 we owed them about £0.5 million secured against the freeholds. Around that time another customer of theirs looked like defaulting on a loan that was a multiple of ours many times over. A new managing director was appointed with instructions to call in all the loans that he could.

We were told that the money had to be repaid and that, if necessary, the freeholds were to be sold. Property prices at the time were in the doldrums and with my knowledge of the market I knew that a turn around would inevitably come and the freeholds would eventually be worth a lot more. But ABN insisted on having their loan repaid. I dug my heels in and tried to find another bank to replace ABN. After a number of false starts we went to Anglo-Irish Bank, who provided us with the facility that we needed. Anglo-Irish was a great bank to deal with and is really *au fait* with the needs of business people.

Our accountant, however, had got a bad fright from the activities of our bankers and convinced Graeme it would be in our interest to sell the freeholds and pay off all our borrowings. I thought this was a very bad idea and for the first time in our business relationship we had a severe disagreement. I argued long and hard that property prices were bound to rise and we would not get the same return on an investment anywhere else. Graeme and the accountant were adamant, however, that this was the proper way forward and that we should not be putting our business and ourselves in thrall to the banks.

Around this time our dear mum died and it was a very traumatic time for all the family. Our Bank of Ireland manager had the gall to attend her funeral and it took all my best efforts to restrain Graeme from making his feelings forcefully known to him. An era had ended and we were on our own. Never again would I have someone to whom I could tell everything and who would listen and be non-judgemental. I had lost a friend as well as a mother. Mum was buried in the Stanley family vault in Mount Jerome alongside my dad, Bonnie. Soon after, I arranged for a plaque to be erected with both their names on it.

After a lot of discussion and argument I gave in and agreed to the sale of the freehold property that we owned in Temple Bar, Baggot Street and Rathmines. We obtained £500,000 for Baggot Street and like amounts for the other properties. I estimate that they would now be worth in the region of £5 million. Because of my property background I had to appoint sales agents and oversee the disposal. It was a very sad time for me. It was made more difficult because Fintan Gunne, the managing director of Gunne Estates, was taken ill soon after he had been appointed to handle the sale of 3 Upper Baggot Street. Fintan, a fellow Rotarian, was a lovely man and died soon afterwards. His son Pat, who now runs the business, has followed in his father's footsteps and is also a member of the Rotary Club of Dublin.

My home life was not much better. Helen and I had been drifting apart for some time. Outside of the family her principal interest was the WPA, which, by definition, I could have no part of. My business life, which involved me having to work late many evenings in the week, was not a good one for a happy and convivial married life. By and large we had plenty of money and were able to go away on lovely holidays but the old spark was gone. The armed robbery did not help matters and was a major factor in our eventual break-up.

One evening I was called into the restaurant at 3 Upper Baggot Street: there was a crisis. The central chimney was collapsing and, as the building had been built using the chimney-breast as the principal support for all the floors, it looked like the building would implode. The problem was in the basement, where bricks had begun to fly out of the chimney-breast structure. When I got there, all that was left to support the building was a thin sliver of brickwork that threatened to collapse at any minute. Something had to be done and quickly. It was an August bank holiday and our regular builder was nowhere to be found. The *Golden Pages* was the only alternative and I eventually managed to contact a demolition expert and a builder, both of whom could come down to look at the job that evening.

The demolition man arrived first and told me I was a fool to be standing in the basement, as the whole place could collapse at any moment. He explained that the chimney-breast was the support for our building and the building next door and that without it number 3 and the adjoining structure would collapse. He quoted £5–10,000 to remedy the situation.

Next on the scene was the builder who took one look at the place and said that I would have no change out of £20,000. I rang the demolition man back and he started making the place safe that night. Two weeks later the chimney-breast had been reinforced and partially rebuilt and we were able to open for business. The cost was £10,000.

There are a couple of odd sidelights to the events at 3 Upper Baggot Street. Next door to us was a shoe-repair shop, which was closed for holidays when the threatened collapse occurred. When its proprietor returned the following week, he got it into his head that I had in some way engineered the near-disaster for my own ends. He had the idea that I wanted to redevelop the site and he would not accept that not only had I nothing to do with the near collapse but also I had in fact saved both buildings due to my timely intervention. We nearly came to fisticuffs on the matter in the street before he finally accepted that I had acted at all times in the best interests of all concerned.

The other unusual aspect was that in the weeks before the near-disaster we had actually purchased the freehold of number 3 for £75,000 and had no insurance for building collapse. We stood to lose everything. A couple of years later we sold the freehold for £200,000, making a profit of about £100,000, allowing for expenditure in the meantime. Not content with that we bought it back for £300,000 a couple of years later before finally disposing of it for £500,000.

On the night of the near-disaster the fire brigade was on the scene and the safe had to be emptied, the staff dealt with and the premises secured.

It was well after 1 a.m. when I got back to Stirling Park. Like on the night of the robbery, the house was in darkness but this time there was no response to my repeated calls. There was no one at home. Helen had gone, taking the children with her. This was the beginning of a nightmare that has afflicted many other men and women in Ireland and abroad. The break-up of a marriage after so many years is not an easy matter. There was a lot of heartache on both sides and invariably, despite our best efforts, our children shared in the trauma. They say that time heals and certainly in my case it has. I have been able to move on with my life and, looking back, I am grateful for the happy times and for our children.

I must be a survivor. Those years were tough and the combination of the hassle from the banks, the arguments about selling the freeholds and the break-up of my marriage certainly imposed a great strain on me at the time. I came through, however, with the help of good friends and because I have an optimistic outlook on life. I was not to know that a new business challenge was just around the corner.

CHAPTER 19

Franchise revolt

B Y 1997 Abrakebabra had opened its 50th restaurant, in Kildare town, and the opening was a big event. The local TD, Charlie McCreevy, who later that year became Minister for Finance, came along to officially declare it open. I had known Charlie from my days with MEPC when he was a chartered accountant with our auditors. Charlie is as straight and honest a guy as you are likely to meet and these qualities have not always been appreciated. He tells it like it is and sometimes people do not want to hear the message.

It was a great day: Charlie did the honours and another friend of mine, the singer Angel Brennan, came dressed as Marilyn Monroe and sang "Happy birthday, Mister Abrakebabra". I had known Angel from my involvement with the Dublin Rotary Club, who organised an annual outing for needy people in the Kilnamanagh Shopping Centre, Tallaght, with the co-operation of Dunnes Stores. Angel, who has her own band and is married to Colm, sang at the party for the participants and in talking afterwards we discovered that we shared a love of gardening. She has a lovely home in Straffan with an acre of beautiful gardens around it. She is a great person to go to for advice and it is wonderful to be able to get a woman's perspective on life's difficulties.

By this time we had restaurants throughout Ireland and had

established a presence abroad also. It looked like nothing could stop our further growth. However, a couple of problems were lurking under the surface that would cause us huge difficulties and heartache over the following two years. These were our company restaurants and a number of severely dissatisfied franchisees.

While we had 50 restaurants, the company owned 10 of them and the other 40 were run by franchisees. Thus, we had to focus on two fronts and inevitably we tended to think firstly about our own restaurants and secondly about our franchisees. In fact when we analysed a breakdown of how our management time was spent we discovered that 60 per cent went on looking after our own 10 restaurants.

The practice had been to have our ten managers into head office every Thursday and carefully go through every figure – gross profit, wages, stock – not to mention any particular difficulty a restaurant might have. It turned into a nightmare situation in that the quality of the managers varied greatly. Half of them were good but the other half would drive you nuts. At the same time the Celtic Tiger was beginning to roar and a serious labour shortage was developing, causing its own problems of supply and demand.

While we focused on these problems, our franchisees, who had their own variant of the same difficulties, came to feel that they were not actually getting the return from their 6 per cent fee that they felt that they were entitled to. Looking back, I can see that they had a point but at the time we tended to adopt a defensive attitude, which did not help matters.

The company restaurants had delivered powerful advantages to us over the previous fifteen years. They had, for instance, been an important source of cash during the development of the franchise business model. They were also an important learning mechanism and through them we were able to gain a practical insight into restaurant management, the impact of design changes, branding, product and service delivery. All of these could be observed and learned from at a practical level in our own restaurants. This, in turn, enabled us to pass on this knowledge to our franchisees and to refine their management-control systems to achieve the optimum return on capital and labour investment.

A financial analysis of the returns from the company restaurants showed that, although 60 per cent of management time was being spent running them, they were, in fact, only breaking even. On the other hand, the franchisees that were getting only 40 per cent of our time were returning a healthy profit. There was something radically wrong and we had to reassess what business we were actually in. Were we in the business of running kebab restaurants or was franchising our core business? It did not take an Einstein to work out that the latter was the case and that we should sell off our own restaurants to franchisees as soon as was practicable.

We immediately set about identifying prospective franchisees to take on our restaurants, many of which were in prime Dublin locations. It took us about eighteen months to secure the sale of all our outlets and in the meantime trouble was brewing among some of our franchisees.

Many expressed concerns over the management of the franchise network while some claimed they were unhappy at the lack of management focus. It also became apparent to us that some franchisees were arranging secret meetings to which the franchisor was not invited. It had been the practice to hold quarterly meetings to which all the franchisees would be invited and at which all issues could be discussed. About this time a number of franchisees were becoming more aggressive and were trying to overturn the franchise agreement and rule by numbers. Their principal complaint was that the franchise fee was too high and should be reduced. These particular franchisees viewed their royalty fee as a cost, while underplaying the benefits that they actually received from the franchisor in branding, central administration and purchasing. They believed that if they could muster an organised attack on the Abrakebabra management team they could have their royalty fee reduced.

We were faced with a difficult decision: how could we quench this revolt without causing major disruption to the company and while keeping valuable franchisees on board. Instead of meeting with the franchisees as a group, we decided that we would arrange individual meetings with each franchisee. This was a very time-consuming exercise but it was a vital strategy in dealing with this serious situation. Through these meetings Graeme and I could clarify in our minds what the situation on the ground was and we could clarify in the minds of the franchisees the value-added contribution of Abrakebabra Ltd. The process of communication with the franchisees proved successful. Most were happy to remain in business and to continue as franchisees, paying the full franchise fee of 6 per cent (net of VAT).

However, a small number of franchisees were not convinced by our arguments. Ultimately, in these few instances, both parties agreed that their relationship was no longer tenable and we decided to go our separate ways. Several of these franchisees subsequently founded their own independent restaurants, some of which did not survive for very long.

The outcome of the franchise revolt was two-fold. The remaining franchisees were satisfied as to the value created by the franchisor and the commitments both financial and managerial that both parties made to each other. And it served to clarify in the mind of the franchisor the value that they brought to the franchise network and the importance of direct, individual communication with their franchisees.

We had gone through a phase where the franchisees were beginning to control our business to a situation where we had reversed the process until we were totally in control of the whole network. The policy was now clear: any franchisee uncommitted to the Abrakebabra ethos, as laid down by us, was offered a release from their contract. From then on, all our dealings with franchisees were on an individual basis. A franchisee that has any issue that concerns them deals directly with Abrakebabra management.

Divesting ourselves of the company restaurants served to strengthen our hand in dealing with the revolt. The new ownership structure forced us to identify a new model for growth. We were leaving the entrepreneurial phase behind and embracing a new control structure centred on a reorientation of our franchising model.

With the exit of some franchisees came the rather belated realisation that the quality of the prospective franchisee would be a lot more important than their quantity. The problem was how to identify the qualities that we required when it came to recruiting new blood. The basic fact of life was that if the franchisee was not making money then he could not afford to pay the 6 per cent fee and we would not be making a profit. As we were now totally reliant on the franchisees, and they on us, this fact concentrated our minds wonderfully. No more company restaurants meant that we had, in effect, no fall-back position. We had to be sure that we picked the right people for the job.

Previously we had chosen franchisees on the basis that they had the necessary financial resources and perhaps a background in the fast-food industry. The last criterion was not absolutely necessary: many people had made a success of the business because they were prepared to work very hard and had the ability to motivate staff and attract customers. In the 1980s we had been inundated with interested candidates and consequently were able to be quite selective in our choice. However, after the trauma of the revolt we set about making the selection process more formal.

We prepared a brochure setting out the responsibilities and advantages of being an Abrakebabra franchisee. Having read that, a prospective franchisee would be required to complete an application form and sign a confidentiality clause, before being interviewed by the franchise director. The interviewer would try to evaluate the applicant's ambitions, intentions and personal characteristics. Abrakebabra was looking for a high level of commitment: we did not want investors but people who were prepared to run the restaurants personally. There had to be hands-on involvement.

The ideal person would be someone with experience in management and entrepreneurship, with an ambition to make money and a passion for serving people. We needed people with ideas and energy who had a strong sense of responsibility to their customers, the wider community and ourselves, not necessarily in that order. A high level of educational qualification was not a prerequisite; rather the best combination would be experience, energy and ambition.

Following selection, training would begin. We have found that the best possible form of training is on-the-job training with another franchisee. A new recruit is assigned to an established franchisee and works their way through all the tasks required until they are capable of operating and managing a restaurant. This can take anything from two weeks to three months. In the mid-1980s when we took over the Upper O'Connell Street restaurant from the Boyle brothers, we inherited, among other things, a huge cavern-like basement that they had fitted out but never used as a restaurant. For years we ran our training school from there but found that nothing could replace the actual experience of dealing with a customer at 1 a.m. in the morning. Qualities such as speed, tact and a sense of humour are best honed in the heat and excitement of real life.

Working as a team, Graeme and I had come through the traumatic experience of the franchise revolt relatively unscathed. Our General Manager David Zebedee was a great help also and at times acted as "go-between". We were determined to build a new model and were young enough to remain optimistic that it would be as successful as the old one. Our new empire was quite different from the old and the changing responsibilities and work practices would take some getting used to. I have always enjoyed a challenge and I looked forward to the demands that the new situation entailed.

CHAPTER 20

Brothers

I SUPPOSE I HAVE always been a workaholic and the Protestant ethos of hard work bringing its own rewards was bred into me from an early age. The idea I had was that if you work hard and play hard, then you are enjoying life. In 1982 when Abrakebabra was founded I was 34 years of age, had loads of energy and was physically very strong. Twenty-two years on, although life's vicissitudes have taken their toll, I still feel that I can take on challenges of both the body and the mind.

I think that I am a straight-talking and honest individual and as an auctioneer I developed a talent for showing this side to people so they would be inclined to trust me to sell their most precious possession: their home. I have always believed that a person has about three to five minutes to sell themselves to another person, whether in business or in private life.

Graeme, on the other hand, is a bit more reserved and takes a while to be relaxed in the company of strangers. Graeme made a lot of friends in Sligo Grammar School and also developed leadership skills there. He has kept in close touch with these school friends, on a personal and business level.

When it came to seeking new sites, knocking on doors and talking to people about what properties might be available, I always did the legwork and the talking. Over the twenty years plus with Abrakebabra, I sold our business ideas to over 75 franchisees. I had to convince these people to trust me and to commit up to £30,000 of their own money to the project. To achieve this level of trust you have to believe absolutely in yourself, in what you are selling and in your ability to carry out the task that you have set yourself.

When the first Abrakebabra opened in Rathmines Graeme was only 24 years of age and had just married Margaret. He was, and still is, a highly ambitious, energetic individual who has all the traits of a young entrepreneur: determination, vision, creativity and an unmoving self-belief.

I, on the other hand, was working for a large and prestigious property company, had qualified as a chartered surveyor and had a young family to support. While my prospects in the property world had not looked too good, given the state of the market, it took a big leap of faith, and a lot of courage, to follow my younger brother into the world of fast food and kebabs.

Graeme was, and is still, a risk taker and both of us accept the commonly quoted analogy for our relationship: Graeme was the "accelerator" and I was the "brakes". We are equally determined and ambitious and the partnership of two different personalities sharing a united vision helped create a highly successful and profitable business.

There is another side to each of us, as there is to most people. Away from business I have always been passionately interested in nature in all its forms. In the mid-1980s I bought a log cabin on a couple of acres in the Glencree valley in County Wicklow. I call it "my thinking place". I go there when I want to get away from the pressures of life or business. There I have the time and space to sit back and work out whatever is bothering me. The setting is conducive to peaceful thought: it has a hive for the honeybees, a tumbling stream runs below the garden and deer wander in and out at will. To complete the natural environment, a badger has made its den underneath the outside toilet. I think it is important to try to achieve a balance in one's life between the pursuit of success and the enjoyment and conservation of the world around us. Butterflies and orchids are my passion and I have travelled far and wide in pursuit of both.

Graeme loves the country life also and lives as a country gentleman in County Kildare. His passion is polo and his string of ponies is his pride and joy. Married to Margaret, they have two boys and a girl. He is very creative, loves designing things and is very shrewd. In fact when Mick O'Reilly, our painter, was finishing the fitting-out of the restaurants he would always increase the price of a job because he knew from experience that Graeme would knock him down a few pounds – he built the Graeme factor into his quotes. Mick's wife, Eileen, acted as our housekeeper for ten years.

I did not like being away from the business for more than a week. I suppose, if truth were told, I am a bit of a control freak. Graeme, on the other hand, having surrounded himself with people he felt he could trust absolutely, could go off quite happily on two- or three-week holidays in the certain knowledge that everything would be fine when he returned. It usually was fine when he returned, largely, I thought, because I had remained behind worrying about the business and trying to head-off difficulties before they occurred.

Because we were 50/50 partners, each of us had a veto on the other partner's wish list. When it came to selling the freeholds I could have held out against selling but I gave in, probably in return for a quiet life. The other major event – the decision to franchise out our own restaurants – was one that I was totally against also. I enjoyed managing our own ten outlets and felt that we kept our finger on the pulse of the business by keeping them under our direct ownership. I agreed reluctantly to the franchising and immediately afterwards was proved wrong. Profits increased and our time was freed-up to deal with the serious issues of running a successful franchise operation. In this case I will gladly acknowledge my own lack of vision. But I still regret selling our freeholds in Temple Bar, Baggot Street and Rathmines.

Graeme was a great person for travelling around the country. We thought that the franchisees deserved to actually see us at least once a month and we tried to visit blocks of six to ten restaurants on each trip. I enjoyed visiting restaurants in the north of the country more than the south because, generally speaking, the franchisees in the northern part of Ireland tended to complain less than their counterparts in the south. They just seemed to be able to run a smoother operation. The trip to Cork, and the south generally, was, to my mind, a bit of a pain in the neck, but a necessary pain nonetheless. The troublemakers, by definition, gave us the most trouble and from an early stage we devised a strategy whereby we concentrated our attentions on them and tried to solve whatever was causing them problems. If that failed we then had to think seriously about eliminating them from the network altogether. The good guys, the ones who ran their restaurants well, needed very little of our attention. The Limerick operation was so well run that we hardly ever had to bother them with a visit.

While I think we were both equally energetic, I feel that Graeme was more driven than I was. He always wanted us to have more restaurants and more success. I would have been content with, for instance, 30 outlets: he wanted 50. I think that he has a vision of Abrakebabra restaurants all over the world and who is to say that it cannot happen.

Although I am the older brother, after a while the partnership settled down into one between equals. Both of us had a lot of respect for the other's qualities and, as we shared an office for twenty years, mostly on an amicable basis, this was quite evident to all that knew us.

We agreed early on that if one of us felt very strongly about something, the other brother would back his sibling all the way. In the beginning it was my job to find the sites and the franchisees and Graeme took responsibility for fitting them out, advertising their existence and dealing with the stock. I dealt with financial matters and Graeme with the actual running of the restaurants and with the suppliers.

As my nearest brother in age, Ian, was not involved with Abrakebabra during the early years that I was there, he has not featured to any great extent in this story. Growing up we were very close, as you can imagine, being only two years apart. There was the usual competition and being the elder I had all the advantages which, of course, I exploited to be always number one. When our dad died and our mum became gravely ill, the responsibility for the family was thrust onto my shoulders. During this traumatic period Ian was a tower of strength to me. I remember clearly both of us packing Graeme's little case as he was setting off to boarding-school. It was a very emotional time for the three of us, particularly as Ian had all the pressures of college life to deal with himself.

Ian graduated from TCD in business studies and after working in private industry for some years decided to follow in the family footsteps and enter the teaching profession. And what better place to find a teaching post than St Andrews College, where his grandmother Eileen Stanley had taught all those years before. Ian left his teaching post in St Andrews in 2002 and is now the health-and-safety manager for Abrakebabra, with responsibility for ensuring that the highest standards are maintained throughout all the franchised restaurants. Ian is married to Joanne and they have three sons and one daughter.

It is very difficult to be accurate about yourself but I will try. The joy in my life has been watching my four children grow and develop. I would say that I am an emotional person but I have had to consciously detach myself from situations on a number of occasions. One of the most difficult things I have had to do in business has been to fire somebody. This is one function that I was happy to delegate to our general managers so that I would be at one remove from it. When we started up we had no buffer between the staff and ourselves and sometimes I had to bite the bullet and do it myself. It wasn't easy.

There are not many brothers who could have worked side by side for twenty years and turn a little fast-food outlet in a south Dublin suburb into an international eating experience. Both Graeme and I have a right to be proud of this achievement and now that Ian is part of the team there is a certain element of continuity. The second generation is also now involved: Graeme's son Stephen, my godson, has taken a franchise on an Abrakebabra in Kildare. Who knows, maybe we will become a family dynasty.

CHAPTER 21

Love affair with nature

ONE OF MY earliest memories of my dad is of being carried over a gate into a field. It is summer, wild flowers are everywhere, birds are singing and butterflies are flitting around us. We are probably in either Donabate or Brittas Bay and the sun is always shining. Away from sport, nature was my dad's other great love. From an early age his father had introduced him to the wonders of nature in the fields surrounding the rectory in Laracor. In later years their relationship had not been the best but as a child my father learned about the different types of birds, wild flowers and butterflies as he and his dad wandered together through the meadows of County Meath in the early years of the twentieth century.

Soon I was able to clamber over the gate myself and, with my younger brother Ian, marched across the countryside with Dad in search of adventure. Butterflies were his passion and in those years we caught them in large nets, put them in a jar with chloroform and mounted them on boards to admire their beauty in glass cases. In the 1955 *Observer Book of Butterflies* that I was given as a seventh-birthday present by my dad I have recorded my capture of one grayling, one tortoiseshell, three fritillaries, three meadow browns, one small white and eight gatekeepers.

At that time butterflies were not in danger from changing

farming practices involving the use of chemicals and the destruction of our hedgerows and it was quite common for little boys to have a butterfly collection. My uncle Tom Corrick, a Chartered Surveyor, who was married to my dad's sister Marjorie, showed me how to make my own mounting boards and how to mount my collection properly.

My dad showed me butterflies mating by joining their tails together, often in flight, and explained to me that they are very particular when it comes to selecting plants on which to lay their eggs. The fritillary will only lay its eggs on the violet, ten different species are attracted by the buddleia, the clouded yellow to clover and the tortoiseshell and the peacock to nettles. In my one-and-a-half-acre garden in Kilternan, where I moved in 1994, I have planted these varieties of plants, together with wild flowers and nettles, to attract butterflies. And the ploy has worked.

Perhaps as payback for my youthful indiscretions, I now am able to breed and return to the wild many types that I formerly captured. With cardboard and cellophane I have constructed a breeding tank and have been privileged to observe one of nature's best-kept secrets: the transformation of a caterpillar into a butterfly. My son Gavin, a budding entomologist, aged nine helps in this work.

The eggs or larvae that a butterfly lays become a caterpillar, feeding on the plant on which it is laid. In time, it sheds its skin and, hanging upside down under a leaf, it hibernates through the winter in chrysalis form. Come the spring it has become the imago or perfect insect. When the time comes to become a butterfly the imago must be hanging freely and have no disturbance. Its wings are pumped up slowly by the insect pushing blood through its veins. I have watched this process many times and have delighted in seeing the newly emerged butterfly taking flight for the first time. I have bred red admirals and painted ladies in

Kilternan and love to watch them flitting about my garden

In nature, as in life, tricks or subterfuge can sometimes make the difference between life and death. Black and yellow are the colours that commonly denote danger in the wild. Coincidentally, governments have now adopted this combination of colours to indicate a nuclear hazard. The caterpillar of the swallow-tailed butterfly, for instance, has yellow and black stripes and the birds tend to ignore it as a potential food source. The peacock butterfly has patterns on its wings that resemble four big eyes. Birds tend to attack these eyes when they swoop in for the kill and I have seen many peacocks with damaged wings because the predator mistook the decorated wing for the real eye.

Butterflies are beautiful insects and with the advent of high-quality digital cameras it is much easier to photograph them and observe their magnificence without damaging them in any way. I have taken many pictures of them and as I write this I am looking at a photo, taken in my garden, of a red admiral with its brilliant wing bars shimmering in the sunlight. Red admirals are living on borrowed time and need to be below the 48th parallel before they can breed. In the autumn you can see thousands drifting south as the summer sun wanes in our latitudes.

The butterfly's wings are covered in overlapping scales, like roof tiles, and their scientific name, "Lepidoptera", is derived from the Greek *lepis*, "scaled", and *ptera*, "wing". Rain can scatter the wing scales and butterflies will not take to the air in wet weather. There are 28 types of butterflies in Ireland while there are over 1,000 varieties of moths. Because moths only fly at night and butterflies during the day this disparity in numbers is not always appreciated.

I have often visited my good friends Ethna and Michael Viney in their home set on one acre at Thallabawn Strand near Louisburgh, County Mayo. Michael has written extensively on butterflies in his "Another life" column in *The Irish Times*.

Among my prized possessions are three line drawings by Michael used to illustrate his series. Some years ago when Shirley and I were fishing for salmon on Lough Corrib, a monarch butterfly actually landed on her and Michael published this sighting in his "Another Eye" section, which runs alongside "Another Life".

One year when I was visiting Michael with my friend Brian "Buzzer" Hughes, we climbed Mweelrae Mountain, overlooking Thallabawn. Halfway up the mountain I came across a perfect specimen of a pyramidal orchid.

I became an orchid lover some years back when I was given a present of a *Cymbidium*. This orchid has beautiful racemes of flowers hanging from green strap-like leaves. I was amazed to discover that the plant stayed in that state for the next three months. And I was further astonished when, exactly one year later, the following December it sent up new shoots or spikes that formed six new racemes of flowers. To find something as beautiful, long lasting and hardy was wonderful.

I discovered later that the *Cymbidium* originates in Tibet and easily withstands the little frost that we get in Ireland. I now have 6 of them, out of a total orchid collection of 300, and they are sitting on a window facing east.

In 2001 I was in the National Botanic Gardens one day and I recognised Brendan Sayers' distinctive voice, even though he was perched on a ladder. We began to talk about orchids and the result was the foundation of the Irish Orchid Society, of which Brendan is now chairman and I am treasurer. The society has 300 members and we publish a newsletter called *Pollinia*. There are field trips to the Burren, Mullaghmore and other sites where orchids are plentiful.

There are about 25,000 different species of orchids in the

world and just 28 in Ireland. A country such as Belize in Central America, which I visited in 2003, has up to 3,000 species and people there grow them in their gardens as Irish people grow daffodils. At any one time, between 30 and 40 of my orchids are in bloom and they make a dazzling and sumptuous addition to my house and garden. I have two green houses and a conservatory full of them.

I have recently learned that the six-spot burnet moth and the common blue butterfly are great pollinators of orchids. They use their tongue or proboscis to probe deeply into the nectar and carry the pollen with them while flitting from plant to plant.

In the nineteenth century Charles Darwin discovered an orchid with a ten-inch long spur with the nectar at its innermost part. He postulated that there must be an insect that can probe into the flower and pollinate it. Forty years after his death he was proved to be correct when the sphinx moth, which has a ten-inch long proboscis, was observed doing just that. I have the orchid in my tropical greenhouse and it is truly magnificent.

Since we moved to Kilternan we have extended the house and added a conservatory and a swimming-pool. The gardens were redesigned with the assistance of Verner Naylor, who advised removing a lot of hedges and positioning paths to give it a greater flow. The soil is acid so I can grow beautiful rhododendrons and vivid blue hydrangeas. We have beech trees that are 200-years-old and oak and chestnut trees that are over 100 years old. I have deliberately not used sprays or chemicals and have instead set up a self-sustaining ecosystem that actually works. Peanut feeders attract birds such as blue jays and long-tailed tits and the over-ripe apples left on the orchard trees are a magnet for jays and jackdaws. The birds feed on slugs and snails and the plants thrive.

Another way in which I have tried to repay my debt to nature and to make up, I suppose, for my childhood activities of raiding birds' nests is through my involvement with Bird Watch Ireland. In the early 1990s my friend Maurice Bryan asked me to become chairman of the Dodder branch of the Irish Wildbird Conservancy. The Dodder River was under threat from the Parks Department of Dublin Corporation, who wanted to cut away all the foliage along its banks and turn it into a canal-like watercourse. A side effect of this would have been that the habitat of the wildlife there would have been removed and the river rendered sterile.

We surveyed the river and discovered that there was a huge wildlife population along its entire length up into the Dublin Mountains. On one stretch alone we discovered 50 nesting pairs of kingfishers. With the help of Evelyn Moorkens, who afterwards, as Dr Evelyn, helped save the fens in County Kildare, we fought the Corporation's plans and succeeded in getting them to agree to respect the habitat of the birds, water fowl, otters and other wildlife along its banks. Another project that the IWC, which later became Bird Watch Ireland, was involved in was the protection of the nesting little terns on Kilcoole beach in County Wicklow. We were able to put wire mesh in place that made it very difficult for foxes to raid the terns' nests, thus providing a sanctuary for the endangered birds.

Partly because of the idyllic surroundings in which we live, my youngest son, Gavin, who is nine years of age, has followed in the family tradition and takes a keen interest in nature. A sika deer gave birth at the bottom of our garden in spring 2004 and both of us were able to observe from a discreet distance the first faltering steps of the young fawn. Gavin has taken after me in other ways too. On holiday in St Tropez he was quick enough to be able to capture a lizard in a jam jar. While admiring his agility, I gently explained to him that he should return it to the wild, which he did. It must be in the blood.

CHAPTER 22

International expansion

BECAUSE WE had been successful in Ireland, we naturally thought that we could bring the Abrakebabra brand to the rest of the world. When you are young and your business concept has been proved right, it is quite natural to think that such an idea would travel. As events were to prove, in some cases it would and in others, where local conditions prevailed against us, it would not.

One evening I was looking at the 9 p.m. news on RTÉ and among other featured items there was the usual Orange Order parade in Portadown in Northern Ireland. I was glancing idly at the screen when my eagle eye spotted something in the background that should not have been there. It was an Abrakebabra sign over a shopfront. We had often talked about expanding into Northern Ireland but for many reasons had not got around to doing anything about it. Although the Troubles were subsiding up there, there appeared to be easier opportunities nearer to home. Anyway, there was no doubt about it: I had seen our name over a restaurant in Portadown and it would have to be investigated. On further inquiry it transpired that an Indian gentleman had set up in business using our name and selling kebabs without asking our permission. It turned out that he did not require our permission because we had omitted to register our trade-mark in the United Kingdom.

We ventured north and had a chat with him and after prolonged negotiations we had to part with £12,000 to buy out his rights. We then registered Abrakebabra in our name and some time later we opened our first franchised restaurant in Derry. Louis McLaughlin was the franchisee. Louis was, and is, a very astute businessman. He was running the Beehive restaurant in the Foyle Shopping Centre and he embraced the Abrakebabra culture wholeheartedly. The first Derry Abrakebabra was on the Strand Road, near the university. Louis subsequently opened a second restaurant in Waterloo Street, with the ancient city walls running behind it. Louis was a great guy and he introduced us to RAP packaging who enabled us to introduce biodegradable packaging into our restaurants and win a BBC environmental award. He also introduced us to Rich Sauces who became our designer-sauce supplier.

Our second restaurant in Northern Ireland was in Belfast. The three Metcalfe brothers, who owned the Beechlawn Hotel, bought out the freehold of a building on Bradbury Place and set up a very successful Abrakebabra. Unfortunately for us, the franchise agreement that we entered into with them was for only five years and at the end of that time they sold the freehold and made a profit of around £200,000 sterling for themselves.

Soon after the Belfast restaurant opened we looked to Scotland for our next venture abroad. We settled on Stirling which, being a university town, had the requisite young population. It is also the hometown of William Wallace of Braveheart fame. We chose our location carefully: right beside the biggest nightclub in the town and an Irish pub that stayed open until 1 a.m. We reckoned that hungry punters would spill out onto the streets after midnight and we would be ready and waiting to feed them kebabs. Unfortunately for us, it turned out we would actually be shut: we could not trade after 11 p.m. In Scotland, we discovered, the licensing laws are different from Northern Ireland, even though both are part of the United Kingdom.

In Stirling the police have control over licences, although you have to apply to a court to obtain one. We went before the judge but the local police objected because they "did not want any trouble". They apparently did not have to adduce any evidence that an Abrakebabra had been the cause of trouble; all they had to do was offer the opinion that they thought people eating after leaving pubs would be troublemakers. As we could not open during our main trading hours, we decided after some months that a restaurant in Stirling was not viable.

Our second venture in Scotland was in 293 Sauchiehall Street in Glasgow. Sauchiehall Street was a long street, famous for having a raft of nightclubs at one end and shops at the other. It was a bit like Lower Leeson Street and Grafton Street in Dublin rolled into one. One of the clubs had the front half of a lorry protruding from its façade, which gave it quite a dramatic look. Unlike in Stirling, we managed to obtain a late-night-opening licence and opened halfway along the street between the clubs and the shops. Unfortunately for us, we did not have the local knowledge that when the punters exited the clubs they headed away from the shopping end of the street. We did have a club situated right beside us but it closed for renovations just after we opened. So even though we thought we had got everything right, the Glasgow restaurant was not a success.

Our London experience was really strange: a guy approached us with bank references for £100,000 sterling, wanting to open an Abrakebabra in Kilburn. I went over to check him out and he met me in his chauffeur-driven car and took me out to have a look at his stud farm. It was really lovely, he seemed to know what he was talking about and he was originally from Ireland. The restaurant was fitted out and we sent a team over to help him get started. After he had been in business for a week, the police turned up, changed the locks on the premises and evicted us. It turned out that he was a complete con man. His car was rented by the hour, he lived in the gate lodge at "his" stud farm and he had omitted to pay key money to the Indian gentleman from whom he was taking over the lease. We dropped about £70,000 on that disaster, not to mention the time and effort we put into setting him up. I do not know how he obtained the bank references: they were the only things that were genuine.

One day I took a phone call from a person describing himself as Sheikh Abul from Bahrain. He told me that he was a member of the Chamber of Commerce there and that his son, an architect, had come across our name while researching franchising ideas on the Internet. As our name, luckily enough, was one of the first in the English alphabet he had found us pretty quickly. I have to say that my initial reaction to the telephone call was one of scepticism. But as I was in the Dublin Chamber of Commerce and sat on its retail committee I was able to confirm, without much difficulty, that the sheikh actually existed and was who he said he was. He told us that he already owned sixteen bank exchange units and two apartment blocks. He was obviously very successful and wealthy. Sheikh Abul had two sons and wanted to build an Abrakebabra on the ground floor of one of his apartment blocks. His plan was that one of his sons would manage it. He had the space and had already obtained planning permission.

At this point I invited Sheikh Abul to come to Ireland and see our operation for himself. I undertook to show him around personally and sure enough he soon arrived for a visit. Sheikh Abul was a very honourable man and liked what he saw in Ireland. He immediately asked if Graeme and I would go to Bahrain, have a look at his site and help him design the restaurant. My answer was that if he paid for our flights and hotel expenses and secured the deal with £20,000 up front we would seriously consider going. He declined our offer.

My knowledge of Bahrain at that time was sketchy, to say the least. I knew it was in the Middle East but that was about it. Before going any further with our negotiations I decided to learn something about the place. It turned out that Bahrain is an island of about 570 square kilometres in the Persian Gulf. In 1985 it had been connected to its nearest neighbour, Saudi Arabia, by a causeway, enabling Saudis to drive over if the urge took them. As Saudi Arabia is completely dry when it comes to alcohol and it was readily available in Bahrain, it seems that the urge took them to Bahrain a fair bit. Bahrain had also been developed as a major trading post and many international financial institutions had a presence there. It had a US air-force base and was home to over 5,000 Irish citizens. The more I learned about the place the more interesting it became, but it was very far away and at the time we were opening an average of about one restaurant a month in Ireland. Both of us were very busy men.

However, I was keen to go. Although we had failed in Scotland and London, the thought of flying the Abrakebabra flag outside the island of Ireland still appealed to me a lot. So we did a deal with Sheikh Abul that he would pay our expenses and come up with a fee of £10,000. We travelled out and were very impressed with the place. The design of the streets, shopping centres, offices and government buildings was state of the art and some of the shops had escalators even though they were only three steps up from the street. We viewed many suitable sites and although the site that Abul had earmarked was not the busiest one it had the advantage of being flanked by residential buildings and apartments. It also had a large shopping area nearby and as it was at a busy cross roads it would be visible to oncoming traffic. We suggested that he negotiate with one of the owners of a nearby apartment building to erect a huge poster on the side of the building. He replied, "Oh, that's fine. I own the building."

While we were there we ate in beautiful restaurants and Abul introduced us to many prominent figures in Bahrain society. He also bought caftans for Graeme and myself. They are very light and comfortable and we have a brilliant photograph of us wearing them.

Back in Ireland we trained Abul's son and he was so proud of being a part of the Abrakebabra operation that he insisted on wearing our uniform as he walked down O'Connell Street. This was quite different from what we were used to, as by now it was hard enough to get our own staff to wear the full uniform in the restaurants, never mind outside. He was a very interesting young man and thanks to that phone call from Abul there are now four Abrakebabras in Bahrain. A plaque to commemorate the opening of our first restaurant features Minister for Commerce Mr Ali Saleh Al Saleh, Minister for Labour and Social Affairs Mr Abdulnabi Al Shoola and Minister for Health Dr Faisal Radhey Al Musawi. The Minister for Commerce was one of the speakers at the function, further evidence of the extent of Abul's influence in Bahrain.

CHAPTER 23

Public and private

THEY SAY THAT an entrepreneur is someone who lives on the edge, enjoys the thrill of deal-making and achieving the victory. By the turn of the century we had 65 restaurants with the Abrakebabra name over their front door. The real challenge now was to increase the business being done by those assets while looking for suitable locations in which to open new outlets.

Through the 1990s the menu had gradually been changed so that by the end of the decade kebab sales accounted for around 27 per cent of the total. The marketing approach had also evolved and we were determined to have a more balanced business with less dependence on the late-night trade. About 50 per cent of our business was being carried on between 10 p.m. and 4 a.m. and, with the economy continuing to expand, it was proving harder to find people to work these very anti-social hours. The influx of non-nationals helped alleviate this problem but we still thought that we could do more business during the day.

Our new menus contributed to this strategy and our lunchtime trade had begun to expand. In addition to baguettes and kebabs, you could partake of steak sandwiches, vegetarian dishes, various burgers and hot dogs, together with tasty extras such as dips, fries, wedges and even fish and chips. Our menu had truly come full circle from 1982 when we set up in opposition to the local chipper.

Over the years our service to our franchise holders has sharpened up considerably. Knowing precisely what is going on in the marketplace and how your experience compares with others' is a vital component of success in business today. As a franchiser, Abrakebabra provides its franchisees with regular global information, including overall market size, sales volumes and market-growth data as well as specific product information indicating which are the best-selling lines.

The introduction of a modem into all restaurants has given Abrakebabra instant access to turnover figures and the ability to spot eating trends as they develop. This important market information is passed back to the franchise holders, enabling them to gear up to cater for the current needs of their customers. Our success has been due to the innovative idea of bringing a new food to Ireland and our ability to sell it to the Irish public. We are continuing to do this and management are always available to provide their franchisees with confidential business-consultancy advice in such areas as the preparation of business plans, correct structure for their business and general management advice.

While some areas in the country still have not had the opportunity to sample our delicacies, these are few and far between. Our Scottish venture was not well thought out but there is little doubt that there are possibilities in the UK and beyond if the proper market and legal research are carried out in advance.

Outside of Abrakebabra, the 1990s were for me, personally, a time for renewal, for recharging my batteries. In 1991 a good friend of mine, Niall O'Donoghue of Donevin Estates, a fellow auctioneer, invited me to join the Rotary Club of Dublin. You will note the word "invite" because you cannot apply to join Rotary but rather a business or personal associate asks you whether you would like to join. Rotary is one of the world's

largest organisations of business people joining together, in
friendship, to engage in charitable works. While it has over 1.25
million members worldwide and 2,500 on the island of Ireland,
it is still relatively unknown.

Founded in Chicago in 1905, the year my father "Bonnie"
was born, by US lawyer Paul Harris, it originally was just a
friendship and business grouping but early on it began to identify social needs in the community. Based on clubs, it spread rapidly throughout America and in 1910 the first club outside the
US was established in Winnipeg in Canada. In 1911 an Irishman,
Stuart Morrow, who had been a member of the San Francisco
club returned to Dublin with the hope of finding employment
for his debt-collecting talents and told his brother-in-law
William McConnell about the new movement. McConnell
interested his friends in the idea and on 23 February 1911 the
Rotary Club of Dublin held its first meeting in Jurys Hotel on
Dame Street. This was the first club in the Old World and all the
other clubs in Ireland, and indeed Europe, can trace their origins
to us. This is the club that I joined.

We meet for lunch every Monday in Jurys Hotel in
Ballsbridge, usually in the Martello Room and plan our charitable and social activities. Early on I became involved with the
international committee of the club and in particular with its
Aqua Box project. The committee was chaired by Paul Luizzi, a
water-treatment engineer, and together with a Rotarian colleague
in the UK he developed a water- treatment kit that can provide
clean water for villages in the Third World whose water has been
polluted. It is particularly useful in disaster areas where it can
provide instant clean water.

The large blue boxes used to filter the water are also packed
with articles of clothing and emergency aid before they are
shipped out. Unfortunately Paul died prematurely and I had to

take over the running of the project. I remember standing up at the pulpit in Dun Laoghaire Catholic church and telling the congregation about Aqua Box. My talk was instead of the usual sermon during mass and I wonder what my father and grandfather would have thought. I like to think that they would have approved, given the charitable nature of the endeavour. Outside the church, Rotarians and my family collected over £10,000, with a similar amount donated in Mount Merrion. A tie-in with Abrakebabra was that we were able to use our sauce buckets, suitably modified, as collection boxes. They are still, to this day, used for the same purpose.

A good friend of mine in Rotary is Allan Kilpatrick, a director of Weirs, the Grafton Street jewellers. Allan was a contemporary of mine in St Andrews College and remembers my dad running up and down the sideline exhorting whatever boy had the ball to pass it to Wyn so I could score the try. I remember this performance myself and it did not make me very popular with my teammates. Allan organises our annual outing to the Rathmines and Rathgar Musical Society and it is always a great night.

Since 2002 I have sponsored the prizes at Rotary's annual Golf Classic held in Dun Laoghaire Golf Club. In 2004 I won the trophy for best putter.

In time I became vice-president of the Dublin club but due to business pressures I had to stand aside. Who knows but that in the future I may be asked to step up to the plate again.

The 1990s was also the decade in which I met my partner, Shirley. Shirley Rosney, who hails from Birr, County Offaly, is one of eight children, like my mother, and was by far the best manager we ever had in Abrakebabra. She joined the company as an ordinary member of staff and after some years was appointed manager of our flagship O'Connell Bridge restaurant. She cleaned it up, both literally and metaphorically, from top to bottom and turned it into our most profitable outlet. Turnover and profit margins were increased and you could actually see the tiles sparkle once Shirley and her staff had finished with them. Month after month she won the best-manager prize and shipped TV sets and video recorders down to her parents in Birr. She won so many TV sets that we had to change the prizes. She was a revelation.

By this time my marriage to Helen had irretrievably broken down. We had agreed to separate and she had received the family home in Stirling Park as part of the settlement.

One day on my rounds of the restaurants, I dropped into the O'Connell Bridge restaurant to carry out my usual checks. I knew that it was Shirley's day off but there she was working away. It transpired that some task had to be done and she had come in to complete it. Given that she was our best employee and was working for us on her day off, it seemed the gentlemanly thing to offer her a lift to her flat in Glasnevin. We took a detour and found ourselves instead walking over Howth Head on a beautiful sunny summer's day. As we settled into the long grass and I looked into her gorgeous big brown eyes, the thought did occur to me that I could be sued for sexual harassment. As delicately as I could, I raised this thorny question only to have it dismissed out of hand. As we became more intimate another thought suddenly occurred to me. Howth was a bird-watcher's paradise and I knew that there were certain to be at least a couple scanning the fields with binoculars. While we were concealed in long grass far away from the public path, we could still be on view to twitchers. I again raised my concerns to Shirley, who dealt with them in the forthright manner that I have come to love her for.

"Let's put on a show for them, boyo."

And we did.

Soon after, we moved in together in Sandymount and then we bought a house at 68 The Palms in Roebuck before settling down in our current home in Kilternan.

As well as her big brown eyes, Shirley has beautiful long legs – so beautiful that she won a diamond necklace for finishing first in the sexy-legs competition in *Social and Personal* magazine. With her jet-black hair (now strawberry blonde) and dark eyes she looks stunning in tight jeans and a leather jacket. There is a big age difference between us, as with my father and mother, but this has only added to our happiness. I get to go to rock concerts that did not exist in Ireland when I was younger. And I got to meet her wonderful, welcoming family in Birr. The Rosneys are steeped in the GAA tradition and as Birr is the hurling capital of Offaly the *camán* rules supreme in the family. Shirley's brother Aidan played hurling for Offaly before dying tragically on the pitch aged 19.

I was particularly attracted to Shirley's strong, independent will that, I think, she inherited from her parents. Her dad, Jim, died early in 2004. Shirley lost a father and I lost a great fishing companion with a talent for one-liners second to none. May he rest in peace. Her mother, Bridie, is hale and hearty and rules her family kindly but firmly. The Rosneys are a lovely family and it is a joy to know them. Her sister Stephanie also worked for Abrakebabra and is now nursing in Dublin. Her brother Arnold is now a priest and I had the honour of carrying the chalice when he was ordained in Birr by Bishop Willie Walsh.

When Shirley and I became an item, as they say, I thought that it was inappropriate for her to continue working with Abrakebabra. Instead we opened a sandwich bar called Subs and Salads in South Anne Street. She ran this successfully for some years before we sold it on.

Our son, Gavin, was born in 1994. He is so fast that his teammates on the Palmerstown DeLaSalle under-tens call him their secret weapon. Unlike his dad's experience, these players actually pass the ball to him and he is their top try scorer. He also plays hurling like his Rosney forebears.

Another highlight of the 1990s was my 50th birthday in 1998. Attended by exactly 50 guests, including the then Minister for Finance Charlie McCreevy TD and the British ambassador to Ireland Dame Veronica Sutherland, it was a wonderful night. The only downside was that in my exuberance to celebrate the event I kick-started my Harley Davidson in the hall and burned a hole in the carpet.

The 1990s was, for me, a decade of change. The business had changed and my personal life had altered considerably for the better. As I looked out towards the new century I wondered what it might hold. I was soon to find out.

CHAPTER 24

Lunch with Graeme

BY 2001 Graeme and I had been in business through good and not-so-good times for nearly twenty years. We had often talked about the possibility of a take-over bid and how we would react to such an offer. Twenty years is a long time to be doing the same thing and when we had divested ourselves of the company restaurants I felt that, to a certain extent, my role in the day-to-day running of the business was lessened. We still travelled together to visit the franchisees but I missed the cut and thrust of running our own restaurants, even with all the inevitable hassle it entailed.

About a year previously we had had a half-hearted approach from one of our franchisees, indicating that he was interested in making a bid for our whole operation. After some discussion nothing more came of it but the approach made us think about what the business might be worth. We came up with a figure of around £8 million – although, as no one was really interested in it, it was just academic.

One day, towards the end of 2000, Graeme invited me to go for lunch with him to Patrick Guilbaud's restaurant, where we had a very pleasant meal in that excellent establishment. It was not unusual for either of us to invite the other out to lunch if we wanted to discuss something away from the office. I was not aware of any pressing topic and as the meal drew to its close I thought that Graeme was probably going to wish me a happy Christmas or some such thing.

We had just finished our dessert when he introduced the topic of the sale of the company. He told me that he had received an offer from someone, unnamed, that I knew and that he was anxious to accept. The deal, however, was conditional on my agreeing to sell my shares to the mystery bidder. To back this up he produced a piece of paper with some details of the offer on it and asked me to sign it.

To say that I was surprised is an understatement: I was totally flabbergasted – both by the manner of the offer and the amount on the table. I rejected it out of hand; we finished our lunch and parted. Although relations between us over the succeeding weeks were a little cool. In the New Year Graeme returned to the topic of the proposed sale. Negotiations took place over the next few months and eventually I agreed to sell my shares for a greatly enhanced offer. The purchaser indeed turned out to be someone I knew: he was Denis Desmond, whom I had got to know when we had had the fast-food concession at Féile. We had also been partners in the River Club.

After twenty years I had severed my connection with a business that had been an integral part of my life, day and night. It was a bit of a wrench but, on the other hand, I was now free to become involved again in my first love: property.

Graeme has continued running Abrakebabra and today it is as strong as ever with 55 restaurants. There will always be challenges to overcome in a business that is, by definition, fast moving but Graeme is ten years younger than I am and well suited to the buzz and excitement of it all.

I now had capital to invest and I looked around for a high-yield property investment that made sense to my MEPC-trained instincts. I have since purchased some high yield properties to keep me busy in the future.

To celebrate my newfound commercial freedom I set off for Canada on a holiday with my sons David and Jeff. We hired a V8 open-top car and travelled from Montreal to Quebec and on up the Saint Laurence estuary to Whale Watch. Our plan was to go whale watching and on the following weekend attend the Grand Prix. We stopped at Talahase, a lovely old Indian trading-post, hired a boat and headed out into the Saint Laurence to see the fin whales. A pod of about a half a dozen whales came by our boat and every six minutes they would surface and blow clouds of mist into the air that enveloped us all. They are magnificent, beautifully streamlined mammals measuring up to 100 feet long and when they roll on their backs their fins pop up, hence their name. We also saw beluga whales, which are white in colour and are afforded perfect camouflage in the winter when the Saint Laurence is frozen. When we saw them in June they were bright white and easily seen.

We eventually got to the Grand Prix where, for some reason Michael Schumacher was surrounded in controversy and the crowd booed him and team-mate Rubens Barrichello when they drove around the circuit in vintage cars before the Formula One race began. It was a great holiday and it was wonderful to be away with my two older sons, to have some quality time together. Shirley had stayed behind with Gavin, but she and I have had some fabulous holidays before and since. This was a time for the boys.

Some years previously Shirley and I had gone on an amazing holiday to Venezuela. We had flown to Caracas and then taken a small aircraft down to the Brazilian border, where we flew over one of the great natural wonders of the world: Angel Falls.

Discovered by Johnny Angel and named after him, the falls are so remote that it took him two weeks to get back to civilisation after his discovery. It truly is an amazing sight, with water pouring off a table-type mountain or *tapui* to the valley floor 3,000 feet below. While we were over the falls we ran into a severe thunderstorm and had to head back to our airstrip as quickly as we could. After we had landed the pilot was kind enough to tell us that if we had been five minutes more flying in the storm we would have had to make an emergency landing in the jungle. Remembering the jungle that I had seen as we flew over it on our way out, I would not have fancied our chances of survival. I think I should add light aircraft to my list of flying machines to avoid.

I have a great love of travel and the sale of my shares in Abrakebabra has allowed me to indulge this to a greater extent than would have been possible had I still had executive responsibility.

I also have more time to spend with my friends. Paul Kerr, who lived next door to my grandfather on Trimlestown Gardens, has been a buddy since childhood. We have a regular golf date and often go hillwalking. A few years ago we climbed Carrantuohill in County Kerry, the highest mountain in Ireland. Also on the climb were Donal McCarthy, Des Kennedy and Pat Twomey. Parts of it are quite steep and Paul swears that at one stage I grabbed his leg and saved him from falling down a precipice. Who am I to doubt his word? Coincidentally, before he moved to Trimlestown he lived as a child on Pembroke Road. His family had a flat in the same large house as my cousin Thekla Beere and the artist Cecil King.

Paul confirmed to me recently what I had suspected for many years: that Thekla and Cecil had been more than good friends. His mother remained friendly with Thekla after they had moved to Booterstown and was often invited to her cocktail parties. It is Paul's mother, who passed away recently, that I am indebted to for confirmation of a rumour that has been going around our family for some time without any corroboration.

Thekla's cocktail parties, as I have mentioned, were occasions when government ministers, high civil servants and artists rubbed shoulders and enjoyed themselves. On occasions like this, you always have someone who knows very little about art but seems determined to prove the opposite by spouting non-sense. Usually such people are indulged and the presence of sufficient alcohol makes listening to them just bearable. Thekla's home was adorned with many paintings and, as most of them were by Cecil King, one was more abstract than the next. I am not a great lover of abstract art: I like, by and large, for a paint-ing to reflect something to which I can relate. But abstract art was what was on show at Thekla's cocktail parties.

At one of these soirées a certain guest was holding forth on the deep meaning of a particular work when the "work" itself opened to admit a tray of sandwiches: it was the hatch to the kitchen. There is no record of how the poseur dealt with this blow to their powers of artistic interpretation but it certainly raised a laugh among the assembled guests.

Paul is a very good golfer and over the years we have had tremendous battles at Powerscourt Golf Club. He is a consistent golfer who plays to his handicap and when I beat him, which I do occasionally, I always know I am playing my best. You have to be to beat Paul.

My newfound freedom has also given me the opportunity to indulge my other passion: cars. All my life I have adored cars, particularly when I could not afford the cars I really wanted. In addition to my Mercedes 350 SL, which I drive on a daily basis, I own a 1991 Ferrari 348 that I bought in London. It has red and cream upholstery and I allow myself a drive in it a couple of times a month. It is not made for Irish roads, being more at home on autostrada or autobahns, but it is still a wonderful car to drive. I also own an MGA 1956 Roadster with all the original fittings, including the Motorola transistor radio. All my cars are kept in pristine condition and are serviced regularly by specialist craftsman James Roe of Roe Autocraft in Naas.

Although at the time I was not entirely happy at the way Graeme approached the matter of my share sale, I can honestly say now that it has been one of the best things that has ever happened to me. The absence of executive responsibility for a large and diverse organisation like Abrakebabra has enabled me to focus my energies on what is important to me: my family, nature and the outdoor life generally. If I were still involved, being the type of person that I am, I would have been too involved and would not have had the time to smell the daisies – or even the orchids. I have the time now and I am enjoying it.

If you started this book at the beginning, you will have noticed that I have not yet been suspended under a canoe with alligators snapping at my delicate parts. The best is yet to come, so read on.

CHAPTER 25

Life after Abra

M Y FIRST IMPRESSION of Belize was the intense, humid heat that hit my face as I stepped down from the plane. American Airlines had brought me here from Miami via New York. I had left Dublin two days earlier. Brendan Sayers of the National Botanic Gardens, chairman of the Irish Orchid Society, had brought me on this adventure, which included a two-day excursion into Guatemala where we saw Mayan Temples and walked on tree-top rope bridges with monkeys calling all around us.

We were to spend two weeks in this magical place. The "holiday" included a three-day trip in canoes up the Monkey River valley, which was dripping with orchids and teeming with wildlife. The valley was due to be dammed and flooded in 2004 to provide a hydro-electric scheme.

My favourite orchid is the fragrant black orchid, *Encyclia cochleata*, that is the national flower of Belize. On our way up the Monkey River we saw this orchid at du Plooy's Jungle Lodge. There were hundreds of varieties of orchids literally dripping from the banks of the river and as we went we collected specimens. Brendan suggested that we store them in our life-jackets so they would be safeguarded if the canoes capsized. We could all swim except our Mayan guide. There were six of us in three canoes and we had to carry the canoes over waterfalls and rapids, wading through the jungle in searing heat.

At night we camped by the river and on the second night I heard a tapir stamping his feet nearby. Next day one of these magnificent beasts swam alongside our canoes for several minutes. We also saw sixteen scarlet macaws, which are almost extinct, flying in pairs.

In all we collected 300 species of orchid and brought them back to the Belize Botanic Gardens. They were kept in quarantine there and later several specimens were sent back to our own botanic gardens in Glasnevin. Among the endangered species that we collected were the *Pleurothallis grobyi* and *Platystele stenostachya*, with many small flowers. We also saw the *Scaphyglottis prolifera*, unfortunately not in flower. One entire riverbank was covered with the purple-flowering *Cattleya bowringiana* orchid. This is the only place that this particular orchid is found in Belize. Growing on the bark of a pine tree were several *Sobralia fragans* with a very delicate scent.

Huge blue morpho and yellow mimosa butterflies, as big as your hands, were flitting about everywhere.

On the way back we encountered real problems. We had collected the 300 specimens, including one unnamed one, and were heading back down the Monkey River when suddenly we came upon unexpected rapids. Before we had time to bring the canoes safely to the bank the surging river swept us along. Completely out of control, we were thrown against some trees overhanging the river and our canoe was capsized. Due to Brendan's foresight the orchids, packed in our life-jackets, were safe and my companion was able to kick his way clear and surface. I, however, again on Brendan's advice, was wearing my hiking boots, which were very suitable for trekking through the jungle but not at all the correct footwear for hanging upside down in a canoe under three feet of water. Because they were so bulky one had got caught under the seat of the canoe and held me fast. It seemed incredible to me that such a strong swimmer as I am should be in imminent danger of drowning, but unfortunately that seemed to be the case. My boot was stuck and, although I kicked and kicked again with my free leg, I could not get enough leverage to free it.

I do not know how long I was under the water but I know that I can hold my breath for about two minutes and I was coming rapidly to the end of my tether. I kicked again, this time as vigorously as I could, and I felt a slight movement of the trapped foot. With one great kick I lashed out against the seat plank, freed my foot and ripped the ligaments in my ankle. I was free but at a price. I surfaced. Everybody else was all right and before long we had reassembled our gear, packed it into the canoes and were on our way. It was not until I had my leg in strapping in the local hospital that I was able to reflect calmly on how I had nearly ended my life by drowning in three feet of water. It is incredible how easily events can overtake you when you least expect them.

We returned safely to du Plooy's Jungle Lodge where we deposited our precious cargo. Having had medical attention for my ankle, I found time to visit the local Rotary club in St Ignacio where I made some new friends. I have always wanted to spend time in the jungle and now I have been able to have my wish. One more of my dreams has been fulfilled, although it was very nearly a nightmare.

Back in Ireland I was amazed to discover that right on my own doorstep a complete field of orchids was under threat. I was alerted to its existence by a neighbour of mine, Lettie McCarthy, the new Labour Party councillor on the local Dun Laoghaire-Rathdown Council.

The field is 40 acres and lies between the Ballycorus Road and Barnasligan Lane, near Kilternan, and contains at least 8 of the 28 orchids found in Ireland. The giant multinational Cement Roadstone Holdings owns the field and when Lettie showed it to me it was one of six possible locations for a landfill site. Some of the orchids include bee orchids, butterfly orchids, tway blade and a three-foot-high spotted marsh orchid. Some of these orchids are in the "Red Data Book" of endangered species.

This is something very special. It is a part of our heritage and the local council was considering placing a dump on something that they should be protecting. As a local resident observed, "It is probably the last wild meadow in South County Dublin."

When I saw the field and learned what could happen to it, I immediately contacted *The Irish Times*, who sent a reporter and a photographer along, and I was featured in that paper on 14 July 2004 standing beside the three-foot-high marsh orchid. I also spoke to the retired High Court Judge Mr Justice Fergus M. Flood who is a member, as I am, of the Stephen's Green Hibernian Club. His advice was invaluable and I led a fight to try to preserve the field as part of our natural heritage aided by Dr Evelyn Mookens and Maurice Bryan of An Taisce. Our case was strengthened when we discovered a natural spring in the middle of the field that fed into the nearby Loughlinstown River which eventually flows into Killiney Bay. Any pollution on the proposed site would inevitably feed into the river, causing serious problems downstream. After a lot of hassle, phone calls and representations we finally managed to save this priceless field from being used as a dump. I am currently negotiating with Cement Roadstone to rent the field, thus protecting this natural wonder for posterity and ensuring that our generation and the generations after us will be able to enjoy nature's beauty in its true open-air environment.

One of my great heroes in the world of nature is Gerald Durrell. He travelled the world collecting species that were in danger of extinction and bringing them back to his zoo in Jersey. There he was able to breed many of these endangered animals and birds and release them back into the wild. When I was in Jersey earlier this year on the trail of my mother Yolande's birth place, in preparation for writing this book, I visited Jersey Zoo, which is a tribute in itself to the great work that Gerald Durrell did for the natural world. There is also a magnificent orchid house there.

Following in his footsteps, one of my ambitions is to go to Africa and visit the gorillas in the mist and maybe, if it was allowed, sit with them for a while. They are so close in the evolutionary chain to ourselves and I believe that we can all learn from each other how to coexist on this small blue planet. I was also pleased that the peregrine falcon has begun to nest again in Glenmalure, County Wicklow, having died out some years ago, probably due to the use of DDT in the environment.

When it came to choosing a title for this book I settled on *A Slice of Magic*. I wanted the phrase to be a play on the Abrakebabra slogan and the fact that the doner was sliced to make the kebab that has been the basis for our good fortune. There is, however, another way of looking at that phrase. All around us in the natural world, whether in the beauty of the orchid or the butterfly, we can constantly observe the magic of nature. To many of us it is just the backdrop to our lives, something we pass by on the way to the train or the shops and do not really see. Throughout my life, walking beside my dad, Bonnie, through the wild meadows of Dublin and Wicklow, I have learned to observe and appreciate the world around me. To me it is not a backdrop to but an integral part of our lives, a part to cherish and take delight in.

To me nature in all its bounty, in all its shimmering beauty, is in itself a slice of magic. Why not go out and savour it, look anew at what is all around us and enjoy the wonderful world we live in.